THE MARLBOR

Some reviews of this book:

'After absorbing this study, it's hard to see what else there is to say about the downs he [the author] so obviously loves... No nook or cranny is left unexplored... It's the perfect companion for anyone venturing out upon the downs today.'

Swindon Evening Advertiser

'You would be hard put to find someone more qualified than Ken Watts to write the first book about the Marlborough Downs... All aspects are lovingly detailed to make this book, as publisher Roger Jones claims: "The last word on the Marlborough Downs for many years to come."'

Wiltshire Gazette

Cover: Marlborough Downs. View east from Milk Hill.
Photograph © Steve Day

Sarsen 'train' – or alignment of stones – on Overton Down

The Marlborough Downs

Ken Watts

EX LIBRIS PRESS

First published in 1993
This revised and reset edition
published in 2003 by
Ex Libris Press
1 The Shambles
Bradford on Avon
Wiltshire
BA15 1JS

Typeset in 10.5/14.5 Plantin

Design and origination by Ex Libris Press

Printed by Cromwell Press
Trowbridge

ISBN 1 903341 15 9

But it is not only documents that are the historian's guide... The English landscape itself, to those who know how to read it aright, is the richest historical record we possess.

(W.G. Hoskins)

Contents

About the Author

Ken Watts was born in Devizes in 1933 and has lived for most of his life in Wiltshire. His interest in local history and topography is long-standing, and since his retirement from his profession of architect in 1989 he has devoted much of his time to this interest.

He has over the past thirty-five years become familiar with the Marlborough Downs by frequently walking them and studying their history. His knowledge was consolidated during a period of several years spent as a part-time warden on the Wiltshire section of the Ridgeway. In addition to writing this book, the author also drew the maps, plans and sketches, and took and processed the photographs.

He has also published *Snap: the History, Depopulation and Destruction of a Wiltshire Village* (1989), *Droving in Wiltshire: the Trade and its Routes* (1990), *Exploring Historic Wiltshire: Vol. 1: North* (1997, reprinted 2001), *Exploring Historic Wiltshire: Vol. 2: South* (1998, reprinted 2002) and *Figures in a Wiltshire Scene* (2002).

The present book is a long-awaited, revised and larger format new edition of a book that has been out of print for many years.

Introduction

When Thomas Hardy revived the obsolete Saxon name of Wessex for the countryside which provided the locale for his books he described it as a 'partly real, partly dream country'. This phrase is equally applicable to the Marlborough Downs which formed part of Hardy's Wessex and are designated the 'Marlbury Downs' on the map which he drew for his novels. The poet Charles Sorley picked up the 'dream' element of Hardy's phrase when he wrote in his poem 'Marlborough': 'I who have walked along her downs in dreams', and Edward Thomas came close to Hardy's 'partly dream country' when he wrote of Richard Jefferies: 'In his home country we are in a spirit land'. There is a magic about this landscape, for the subtle downland is redolent of the distant past. Prehistoric man has left his mysterious marks and monuments upon the surface of the Marlborough Downs which are, in the words of their native writer Richard Jefferies 'alive with the dead'.

My concern in this book has been to include new material wherever possible, and not dwell on subjects which have been extensively covered elsewhere. The late W.G. Hoskins recommended that in order to know a landscape it is necessary to 'get away from the guide-book show places' and I am aware that many visitors to this area restrict their visit to Avebury and consequently fail to experience the many other attractions of these Downs. This book is therefore selective rather than comprehensive. Some important subjects – such as Avebury – have been deliberately treated superficially because a considerable literature already exists. Other less important but interesting subjects have been given wide coverage. I hope that this will tempt some readers into the less-frequented parts of the Marlborough Downs, using this book to provide them with background information which may add to their enjoyment.

It is a surprising fact that no previous book has taken the Marlborough Downs as its subject. H.W. Timperley wrote *Ridge Way Country* in 1935, but his book was concerned only with that part of the Downs associated with the Ridgeway, and A.R. Stedman's *Marlborough and the Upper Kennet Country* (1960) paid little attention to the Downs. The best introduction written to date is contained within the biography *Richard Jefferies: His Life and Work* (1909) by Edward Thomas, a fine writer who was a connoisseur of English landscape and had an intimate knowledge of these Downs which he knew from childhood. Today, eighty-four years after it was published, his first chapter, headed 'The Countryside of Richard Jefferies', provides an admirable short introduction to the landscape of the Marlborough Downs.

Some of the 'real' elements of these Downs today strike a jarring note, as for example when you look north from their northern edge across the motorway to the immense and continuing expansion of Swindon; when you meet – as I have – a rally of a hundred and fifty motor cycles on the Ridgeway; or when you join the 'madding crowd' of visitors to Avebury on a summer bank holiday afternoon.

This book tries to evoke the elusive character of the Marlborough Downs by describing their geology and topography, and relating their history. It describes – to use the words of W.G. Hoskins – 'the observables ... and the secret history that lies behind them'. In the interest of saving space I have sometimes used six-figure map references to define location of remote places, but such references have been generally restricted to places and place-names which do not appear on the current Ordnance Survey Landranger 1:50,000 maps.

My thanks are due to the following. First to the many people with whom I have walked and talked in the Marlborough Downs; to the staffs of Wiltshire Record Office and the Local Studies Library at Trowbridge for their unstinted help; to John Hazel who read this book in first draft and encouraged me with his opinion that it was worthy of publication: and finally to my publisher Roger Jones who accepted this book for publication within three days of first seeing the script.

Ten years have elapsed since this book was originally published and it remains, as was indicated on the original back cover, 'the first to take the Marlborough Downs as its subject'. This improved and larger format edition has been revised where necessary to update it, and the opportunity has been taken correct any minor errors which appeared in the first edition.

Ken Watts, Trowbridge, Wiltshire, March 2003

1 Limits and Geology

'Wiltshire is the node and focus of the chalk' wrote H.J. Massingham. More than half of Wiltshire lies on the chalk which is in two areas separated by the Vale of Pewsey which extends from near Devizes east to Burbage. South of The Vale lies the chalk plateau of Salisbury Plain, and immediately to its north are the Marlborough Downs, which extend north and west of Marlborough and are less extensive than The Plain. The Vale of Pewsey separates North Wiltshire from South Wiltshire, Avebury from Stonehenge, Marlborough from Salisbury, and the Marlborough Downs from Salisbury Plain.

This book is about neither the town of Marlborough nor its district in general. As its title indicates, its subject is the Marlborough Downs and in particular their topographical and historical aspects. These North Wiltshire Downs are more undulating and interesting than Salisbury Plain which suffers from having been blighted by military occupation for most of this century. Access by public rights-of-way to the Marlborough Downs is particularly good, and Chapter 10 of this book suggests a number of walks which provide a very good impression of the character of this countryside which Richard Jefferies suggested offered 'the best walking in the world'.

All the sites and field monuments which are described are readily accessible by public rights-of-way unless otherwise indicated, and the Marlborough Downs contain the finest concentration and variety of prehistoric field monuments in Wessex, and probably in Britain.

Limits

The geographical limits which have been adopted for this book are as follows. The northern boundary is taken as the villages of Wroughton, Chiseldon and Liddington a little south of Swindon. To the east Aldbourne Chase is included as far as Aldbourne and Ramsbury. The southern limits

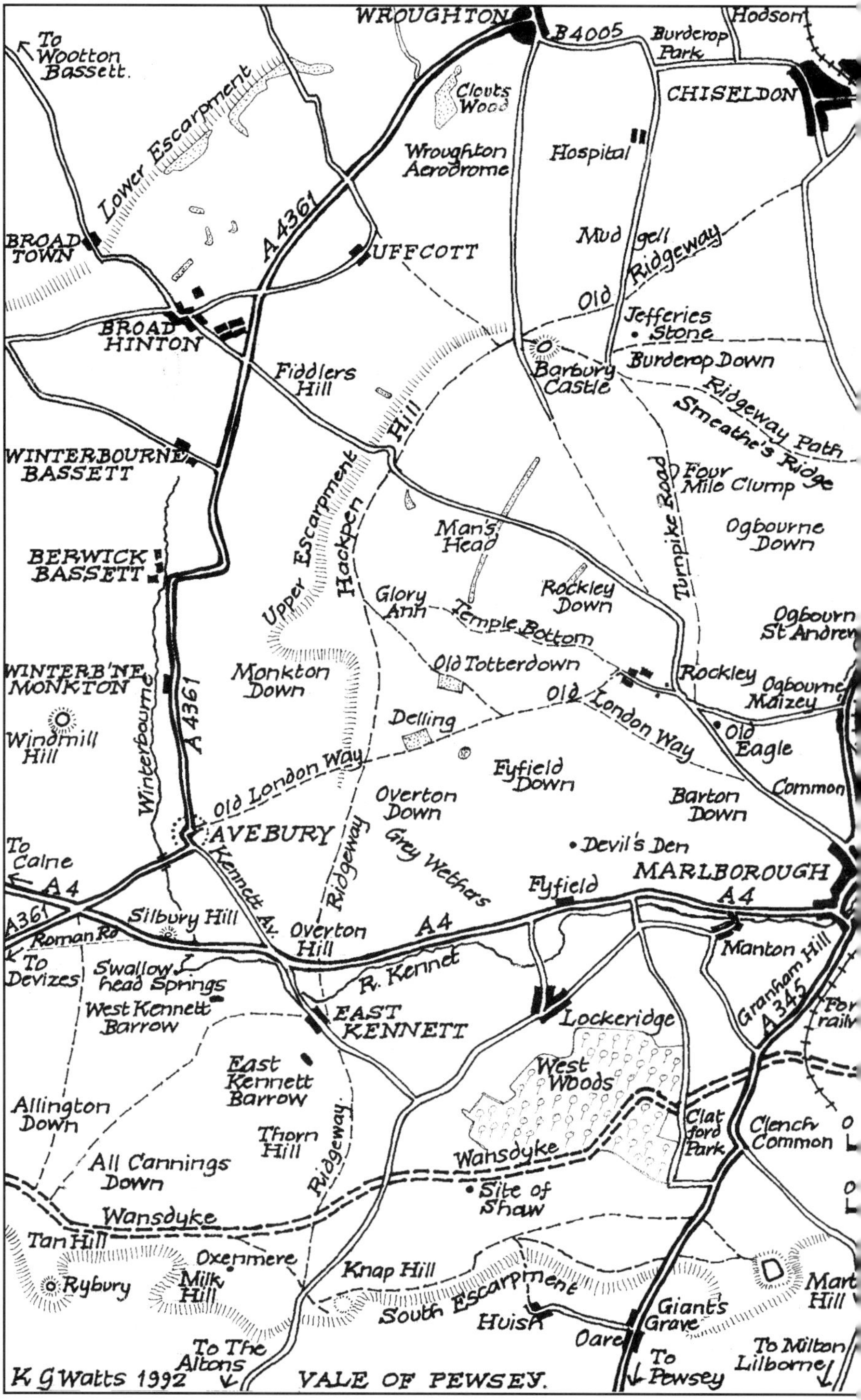

WROUGHTON
B4005
Burderop Park
Hodson
CHISELDON
To Wootton Bassett.
Lower Escarpment
Clouts Wood
Wroughton Aerodrome
Hospital
A 4361
BROAD TOWN
UFFCOTT
Mud gell
Old Ridgeway
BROAD HINTON
Jefferies Stone
Barbury Castle
Burderop Down
Fiddlers Hill
Ridgeway Path
Smeathe's Ridge
Hill
WINTERBOURNE BASSETT
Four Mile Clump
Upper Escarpment
Hackpen
Man's Head
Turnpike Road
Ogbourne Down
BERWICK BASSETT
Glory Ann
Rockley Down
Temple Bottom
Ogbourn St Andrew
WINTERB'NE MONKTON
Monkton Down
Old Totterdown
Rockley
Ogbourne Maizey
Windmill Hill
Winterbourne
A 4361
Delling
Old London Way
Old Eagle
Old London Way
Fyfield Down
Overton Down
Barton Down
Common
AVEBURY
Ridgeway
Grey Wethers
Devil's Den
To Calne
A 4
Kennett Av.
Fyfield
MARLBOROUGH
A4
A361
Silbury Hill
Roman Rd
Overton Hill
A 4
Manton Hill
To Devizes
Swallow head Springs
R. Kennet
Granham Hill
West Kennett Barrow
EAST KENNETT
Lockeridge
A 345
East Kennett Barrow
West Woods
Allington Down
Thorn Hill
Ridgeway
Clatford Park
Clench Common
All Cannings Down
Wansdyke
Site of Shaw
Wansdyke
Tan Hill
Oxenmere
Knap Hill
Rybury
Milk Hill
South Escarpment
Huish
Giant's Grave
Martin Hill
Oare
To The Altons
To Pewsey
To Milton Lilborne
K G Watts 1992
VALE OF PEWSEY.

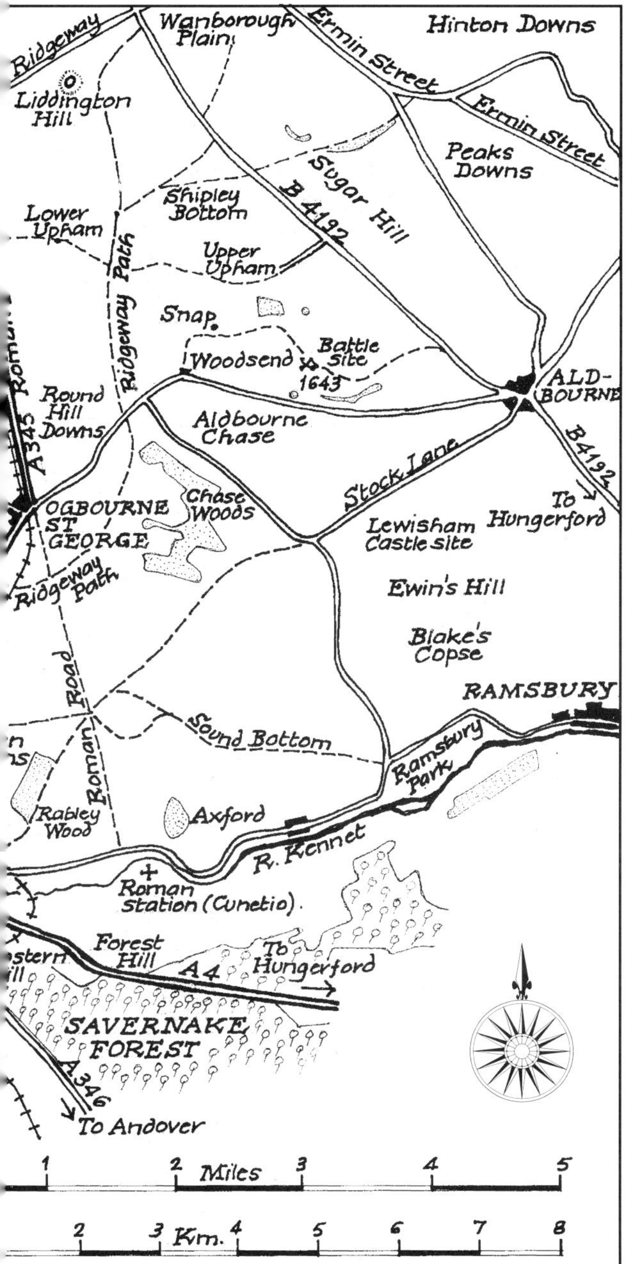

Sketch Map of the
MARLBOROUGH DOWNS

are positively defined by the north escarpment of Pewsey Vale. The western edge of the area under discussion has been taken as the A4361 road which runs along the shelf between the lower and upper escarpments of the Marlborough Downs from Avebury to Wroughton. The Downs west of Avebury towards Devizes – West Down, Cherhill Down, Calstone Down and Roundway Down – have been excluded as I prefer to restrict my book to the main mass of the Marlborough Downs south of Swindon.

The area thus defined is a rough circle ten miles in diameter and enclosing about eighty square miles. It is divided geographically into three areas. The southern section is south of the River Kennet and north of the Vale of Pewsey, the central is north of the Kennet and west of the River Og, and the north-east section is east of the Og and west of Aldbourne.

The southernmost of these three sections south of the River Kennet contains a magnificent area of downland including the scalloped scarp which fronts on to the Vale of Pewsey, behind which lies the site of the deserted village of Shaw. The area north of the Kennet and west of the River Og is the true heartland of the Marlborough Downs. Within this central section are to be found many of the great archaeological monuments such as Avebury, Silbury and Barbury, the great concentration of sarsen stones in Clatford Bottom running up to Fyfield and Overton Downs, the Ridgeway following the long arc of Hackpen Hill, and the living downland village at Rockley. The third area east of the Og consists of that area of the Marlborough Downs which extends towards the White Horse Downs, formerly the Berkshire Downs. This section includes fine hills in Liddington and Sugar Hills, together with the broken terrain of Aldbourne Chase and the sites of former upland villages at Snap and Upper Upham.

Since the word 'Down' seems to be singularly inappropriate for an area of chalk uplands, the derivation of the word must be mentioned. 'Down' is derived from the Old English 'dun' meaning hill. In the Middle Ages this became 'doun' and was applied to all undulating sheepwalks, and in later times this became 'down' as used today.

Geology

The nature of a landscape is inevitably dictated by its geology. The underlying bedrock of the Marlborough Downs is a uniform chalk, which

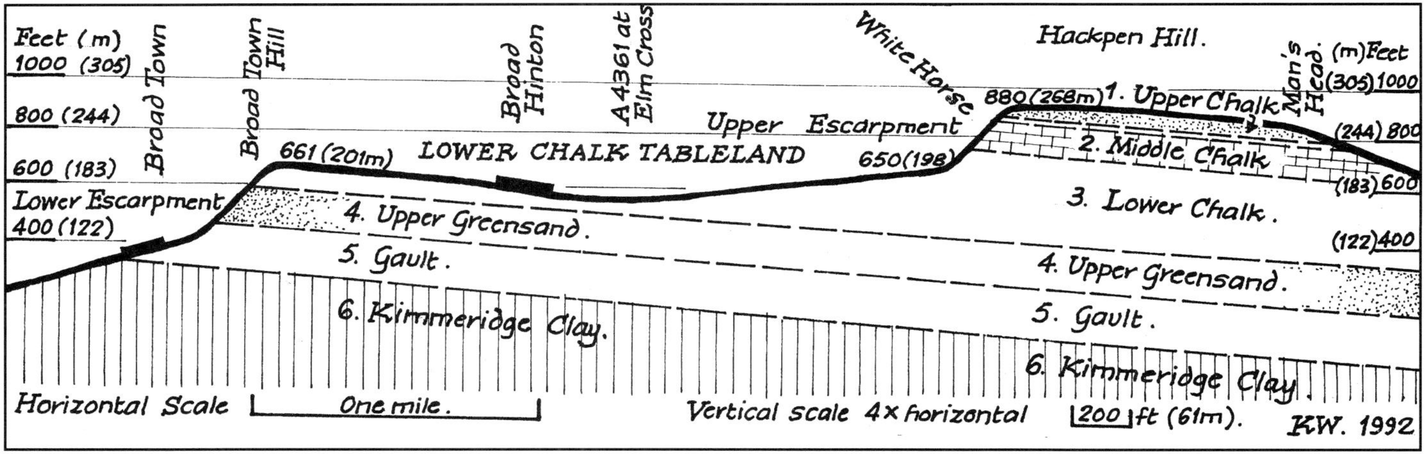

Geological section through the west escarpment of the Marlborough Downs along a line of the minor road from Broad Town through Broad Hinton to Hackpen Hill.

1. UPPER CHALK – soft with many flints (between the Upper and Middle Chalk a layer of chalk rock about 2.5 metres thick which provides chalk blocks, or clunch, for building).
2. MIDDLE CHALK – hard with some flints.
3. LOWER CHALK – mixture of chalk and clay, compact and marly.
4. UPPER GREENSAND – sand grains mixed with other components.
5. GAULT – clay below Upper Greensand.
6. KIMMERDIGE CLAY – dense and impervious.

The strata are gently inclined towards the south-east.

is the purest form of limestone, generally under a thin layer of topsoil. The softness of the chalk explains the rounded character of the Downs for chalk is easily eroded and chalk hills are consequently much smoother in outline than the more craggy hills of stone districts. Critics of downland scenery have sometimes disparaged it as tame compared to the more spectacular hills of the stone districts, but it is my experience – and I have heard this belief expressed by others – that the subtlety and austerity of downland landscapes enter the blood of many of those who frequent and become familiar with them so that they have no wish for more dramatic landscapes. H.J. Massingham expressed such feelings admirably when he wrote: 'In the composure and austerity of the chalk uplands, the very thought of more spectacular country is a weariness'.

At Totterdown and Glory Ann beside the Ridgeway, and at West Woods, Clench Common and on Martinsell Hill, the chalk is overlaid with a layer of loamy reddish clay-with-flints which, being slightly acid, generates a different flora from that which is usual on chalk downlands. On this clay capping grow woods and tree clumps, and at Old Totterdown the unusual sight of rhododendron growing on the top of a chalk down may be seen.

Many chalkpits and quarries, from which hard chalk was excavated for farm tracks and chalk blocks for building, remain in the Marlborough Downs. At Ogbourne St. George a large expanse of bare chalk is exposed in the remains of the quarry of the former lime works (207 738) beside the track which runs uphill to Yielding Copse. An example of a smaller chalkpit may be seen scooped out of the west edge of the Monkton Down promontory from Hackpen Hill (at 116 727), at the end of the lane past Windmill House which provided access to the chalkpit.

Sarsen Stones

The sarsen stones which litter many parts of the Marlborough Downs as surface deposits are of siliceous sandstone naturally deposited in an otherwise chalk (limestone) district. They are extremely hard and are said to have derived their name from the Saracens, an alien people, although they may equally get their name from the Anglo-Saxon 'sar stan' meaning 'troublesome stone', for they were an undoubted hindrance to cultivation. If the name did indeed derive from Saracen, it is of interest to speculate whether this was connected with the Knights Templar presence in Temple

Bottom, since the Knights Templar were a religious order of militant knights formed to fight the Crusades against the Saracens. Sarsens also became known as 'grey wethers' from their resemblance in poor light to sheep on the Downs. This name was accepted by the Ordnance Survey and appears on the current maps.

Sarsen stones have been used since Neolithic (New Stone Age) times for a variety of purposes. The Avebury Stone Circles and most of Stonehenge were constructed of large sarsens, as were the portals and chambers of long barrows such as West Kennett and the standing stones which were erected sometimes isolated and sometimes in long avenues. Broken up sarsens continued to be used as masonry in most periods until modern times and many villages of this area are built of sarsen stone rubble.

In the mid-nineteenth century the Buckinghamshire sarsen masons including the Free family, who in Buckinghamshire had to excavate to

Sarsen stones at the head of Clatford Bottom near Delling Copse. It is said that before the sarsen cutters depleted the sarsens it was possible to walk the two miles from near Delling to the main road at Clatford stepping from sarsen to sarsen.

depths up to twelve feet for their stone, heard of the surface deposits in the Marlborough Downs and moved into the area. They exploited the sarsen stone for about a hundred years, perfecting the art of splitting and squaring it, so that sarsen was used instead of granite setts to pave the Swindon tramways. It is said that the buildings of the Avebury area may be roughly dated from the nature of the sarsen used, random rubble being pre-1850 and square blocks post-1850.

The last major order for sarsen stone from the Marlborough Downs occurred in 1938 when four cart-loads were sent to Windsor for the repair of Windsor Castle. The stone used to be sent to Honey Street by cart and from there by canal barge, the carts returning from the canal wharf laden with coal for the Kennett villages. The sarsen cutters tended to die young from a combination of silicosis and prolonged exposure to the rigours of downland weather, as their graves in the local churchyard testify. An example is the headstone of Edward Free (1830-1875) in Fyfield churchyard. Other masons who died early include Charles Waite aged 45, Henry Waite 42, Frank Kemmer 50, and Walter Bristow 48.

Maps showing the distribution of the sarsens in 1841 and 1941 in the *Wiltshire Archaeological Magazine* (WAM 63) show how much the deposits were depleted over a hundred years by the demands for paving and building. These maps show the main concentrations on Fyfield Down, Overton Down, Clatford Bottom, Pickledean, and West Woods. Often the stones were dragged to the edges of the fields to clear the ground for agriculture resulting in linear alignments of recumbent stones which became known as sarsen 'trains' which are best seen on Overton Down.

The composition and appearance of sarsen stones varies considerably. Some are a kind of puddingstone conglomerate naturally cemented together; these tend to be whitish in colour. A redder form has a high iron content and is most usual in the acidic clay-with-flint areas. Many are perforated with holes which were occupied by tree roots before natural cementation occurred. Depending upon their composition some sarsens split readily into blocks, but others resist splitting and fracture irregularly. This explains the number of sarsens which have been worked on by the masons and then abandoned. On Overton Down (at about 133 704) a sarsen stone may still be seen with a metal splitting wedge still embedded in its top surface, and many others have straight splits showing the marks of splitting wedges at about twelve inch spacings. In fact many of the sarsens on Fyfield and Overton Downs have been moved by man at some time in their history and one very large one on the valley floor south of Delling Copse (at 133 705) looks as though it could for some reason have been abandoned on its way to Avebury.

Building Materials

Sarsen stone was also used until comparatively recent times as gateposts and rubbing stones for cattle. There are many examples of both in the Marlborough Downs.

Buildings are of no particular relevance to a book on the Marlborough Downs, but they do appear as field barns and other farm buildings in even the remoter parts of the Downs. In former times, before the advent of cheap forms of transportation, buildings were constructed of indigenous local materials which are naturally closely related to the geology of the district. In the Marlborough Downs traditional buildings were of sarsen, clunch, cob, brick, flint, a little local building stone, and thatch.

Throughout history extensive use has been made of sarsen stone as a building material, although in the present century it has been discovered that lime mortar must be used, as cement mortar will not adhere to sarsens. Another local building material is the hard chalk from the lower levels known as clunch. This is a rather unpredictable building material, and to be certain of its performance clunch was exposed for a winter before being used to ensure that it was resistant to lamination as a result of frost action. Clunch masonry, often mixed with brick or sarsen, may be seen in many places in the Marlborough Downs, for example at Southend and in The Henge Shop at Avebury. Often sarsen was used at the base of a clunch wall to provide protection against rising damp.

Sometimes walls were shuttered and a wet mixture of chalk, clay and straw known as cob was compacted in the shutters to form building or garden walls. Such walls needed a good capping of thatch and an impervious base of sarsen – 'a good hat and boots' – to survive. Thatched wall-copings were laid upon timber framing which formed the necessary slopes. Ralph Whitlock has recorded that the timber used for this framing traditionally was: 'Always abele, Nothin' else will do' – 'abele' being poplar. A fine example of a thatched cob wall may be seen on the south side of the A4 at West Kennett.

The clay-with-flints which overlays the chalk on some of the hilltops was sometimes exploited for brickmaking, and brick kilns are shown on the old maps (Andrews and Dury, 1773, and the first edition Ordnance Survey of about 1820) at New Totterdown east of the Ridgeway on Hackpen Hill. The fact that Delling Cottage (136 713) in its remote position a little south of New Totterdown is partly clad with tile-hanging suggests that tiles may also have been made at New Totterdown, and it is possible that the brick houses at Avebury are built of Totterdown bricks. The first Ordnance Survey also shows brick kilns on the west side of Round Hill Downs east of Ogbourne St. George.

Although bands of flint are common in the upper chalk and flint pits were dug throughout the Downs, flint was used principally as road surfacing in the days prior to the introduction of tarmacadam. Its use as a building material was restricted, although examples do occur. Some remote field barns were built of flint because this material was readily available on site in the remote upland areas in which such barns were built. Examples of flint buildings include St. Andrew's Church at Ogbourne St. Andrew, Ogbourne Maizey Jacobean manor house – of banded flint and stone – and Rockley Church, built in 1872 of chequered flint and stone. Where flint is used as a building material it is usually reinforced with string courses and quoins of brick or stone.

The nearest available building stone to the Marlborough Downs, apart from chalk clunch, came from the small Portland and Purbeck stone outcrop at Old Swindon, which was exploited from Roman times as a building material.

The traditional and formerly almost universal roofing material in this area was thatch which was used for farmhouses, cottages, farm buildings and barns, walls and ricks. Rockley survives as a partly thatched village, although some slate and tile has been introduced, and the now deserted villages of Shaw and Snap would have been thatched, as would the early village at Upper Upham; modern roofing materials have been introduced on the new buildings at Upham. Thatch is aesthetically pleasing in downland districts partly because of its subtle colour but mainly because the softness at the edges of a thatched roof echoes the roundness of the Downs. The great practical virtue of thatch is its insulating qualities which make it comfortable to live under since it makes the house cool in summer and warm in winter. Thatch is an indigenous material which was cheap because its straw was the by-product of the wheat crop, but today it has become an expensive and fashionable roofing material. This fact has led to many formerly thatched buildings being demolished to avoid the cost of re-thatching. Others – especially field barns – have been re-roofed with cheap materials such as asbestos cement or corrugated iron.

Thatch, clunch and sarsen. The gamekeeper's cottage which was the home of Edward Haylock who inspired Richard Jefferies's The Gamekeeper at Home. *It was described by Edward Thomas as 'the cottage with the thrice-scalloped thatch in Hodson Bottom, sweet chestnut behind it, and birch and spruce at each side: date 1741'.*

The Marlborough turnpike climbing Burderop Down through prehistoric field systems and past a Medieval enclosure (left).

2 The Downland Scene

Until about two hundred years ago the majority of English people lived and worked in the countryside. It may therefore be an element of heredity which explains the fond feelings that most people have for the countryside, and one of the features of the landscape which they most admire is its hills. This affection and recognition of the permanence of hills is reflected in the expression 'as old as the hills'.

From earliest time man has resorted to the high places, no doubt at first for the security which they offered. Prehistoric man populated the hill-tops, and this fact is very evident in the Marlborough Downs. It was the Saxons and their successors who effected the move into the valleys, but there was a tradition which persisted well into the nineteenth century for processions of villagers to resort to their local hilltop to take part in frumenty celebrations at Easter, and stock trading fairs together with their associated amusement fairs were also held on hilltops from earliest times, the classic Marlborough Down example being Tan Hill Fair. There were also celebrations on Silbury Hill and Martinsell.

It is by no means easy to put into words the feelings of exhilaration which are aroused by climbing to the top of a hill and enjoying the view. The act of climbing seems to elevate the mind as well as the body, as Richard Jefferies found when as a young man he used to frequent Liddington Hill from his home at Coate near Swindon. Jefferies believed that: 'The air of the hills enriches the blood', and his admirer W.H. Hudson wrote: 'once we have got above the world, and have an unobstructed view all round, whether the height above the surrounding country be 500 or 5,000 feet, then we at once experience all that sense of freedom, triumph, and elation which the mind is capable of'.

There is a mysterious magic about downland that prompted Celtic folklore to suggest that the hills were hollow and were inhabited by fairies

('How beautiful they are, The lordly ones, Who dwell in the hills, In the hollow hills'). In the context of fairies inhabiting hills, Aubrey tells the story of a shepherd who was lured by a fairy fiddler to a place below Hackpen Hill which resounded with music. I must admit to never having had such an experience, but the area between Hackpen Hill and Broad Hinton is known, and marked by the Ordnance Survey, as Fiddler's Hill. Psalm 121 begins: 'I will lift up mine eyes to the hills, from whence cometh my help', and Shakespeare emphasised the proximity of the hills to heaven when he wrote of: 'hills whose heads touch heaven' (Othello) and of 'A heaven-kissing hill' (Hamlet). The 'green hill far away' of the favourite Easter hymn also comes to mind, as does the fact that public executions took place on hills until well into the eighteenth century, and were the excuse for much merrymaking.

Anyone who would seek the spirit of Wiltshire must walk her Downs which are the true heart of the county. Modern travel routes follow the valleys so that except for recreation we do not now normally follow the upland ways which were the communication routes of early man. Many of the hills of the Marlborough Downs are accessible by car but they are best approached on foot. 'Only the wanderer, knows England's graces' wrote the Gloucestershire poet Ivor Gurney, and Richard Jefferies wrote: 'They only know a country who are acquainted with its footpaths. By the roads, indeed, the outside may be seen, but the footpaths go through the heart of the land'.

It is evident that throughout history the hills were of great significance to man, even though at times he feared wild countryside. The Medieval mind had an innate fear of wild untamed landscape which it regarded as fearful and abhorrent. Such feelings were reflected in the formal nature of Medieval gardens. This attitude continued into the eighteenth century when the typical attitude to downland landscape was recorded by the Rev. William Gilpin (1724-1804) who always disparaged downland and gave as his opinion that 'chalk spoils any landscape'. Of the Marlborough Downs in particular he wrote in 1770: 'Marlborough-down is one of the most dreary scenes, which our ancestors, in the dignity of a state of nature, chose as the repositarium of their dead. Every where we see tumuli, which were raised over their ashes'. Parson Gilpin was however a rather strange man who, having dedicated his last book to the 'memory' of his living wife, predeceased her. The wife then proceeded to publish the book complete with the dedication to her own memory!

At that time, and up to the industrial revolution, man lived an unsophisticated existence close to nature and had no need to cultivate feelings for wild landscape. Today urban man, detached from rural life, feels an instinctive need to devote much of his leisure time to enjoying wild elemental landscape. The periodic 'return to nature' movements have been subjected to a great deal of derision, but such experiences are probably necessary for man's well being, and lack of them may explain the wave of vandalism and crime which has become such a disturbing feature of our society.

It was Professor Hoskins who suggested that 'poets are the best topographers' and for a general introduction to the hills which are the glory of the Marlborough Downs one can do no better than read the poet Edward Thomas who was familiar with this country. He expressed his profound feelings for the Marlborough Downs when he wrote in his biography of Richard Jefferies:

> The Downs in this immediate country of Richard Jefferies are among the highest, most spacious, and most divinely carved in rolling ridge and hollowed flank, and their summits commune with the finest summits of the more southerly downs – Inkpen, Martinsell, Tan Hill ... Jefferies often thought of the sea upon these hills. The eye sometimes expects it. There is something oceanic in their magnitude, their ease, their solitude...They are never abrupt, but, flowing on and on, make a type of infinity ... they have a hugeness of undivided surface for which there is no comparison on earth.

'A type of infinity ... a hugeness of undivided surface'; what better words could be found to describe the scale of the Marlborough Downs?

South Escarpment

The essence of this countryside is its hills, of which Ralph Whitlock wrote: 'Their silhouettes cut the sky more daringly, their slopes are steeper (some are nearly perpendicular), and their altitude is greater' than those of Salisbury Plain. Generally the landscape of the Marlborough Downs is gently undulating with often-dry coombes penetrating deep into the Downs which are surmounted by summits which are especially dramatic at the south escarpment which faces south over the Vale of Pewsey. Here the range of hills is scalloped in both plan and elevation with the promontories of Clifford's Hill, Walker's Hill, and the Giant's Grave spur of Martinsell thrusting boldly south into the valley, their summits undulating, and at Tan and Milk Hills reaching an elevation of 294 metres which makes them the highest hills in Wiltshire. The sequence west to east of this escarpment – which is best seen from Broadbury Banks on the opposite side of Pewsey Vale from where the magnificence of the entire range can be appreciated – is Tan and Clifford's Hills, Milk Hill, Walker's Hill, Knap Hill, Golden Ball Hill, Draycot Hill, Huish Hill, Oare Hill and Martinsell. In his book, *The Wisdom of the Fields*, H.J. Massingham described this range:

> One of the purest landscapes...is the edge of the Vale of Pewsey between Alton Priors and Allington, backed by the long line and masterly modelling in the col, headland and saddleback of the Marlborough Downs...The long barrow of Adam's Grave forms one slope of a green conical mound and below it the land falls away to a wide terrace supported by flying buttresses on two sides.

Since Morgan's Hill, Roughridge Hill and Easton Hill are outside the limits which I have defined for this book, Tan Hill is the first of this range to be described. 'Tan' is a long-standing corruption of St. Anne's Hill, as mentioned by John Aubrey (1626-1697): 'On St. Anne's Hill, vulgarly called Tan Hill, every year is kept a great fair within an old camp...the commodities are sheep, oxen, and fineries'.

This fair was held from at least the fifteenth century until 1932. Aubrey was mistaken in thinking that it was held 'within an old camp' and was probably confused by the linear earthwork of Wansdyke which crosses Tan Hill beside the fair site and was for long used as a traffic route to the fair because it defined the way for strangers coming from afar. There was formerly a barn beside Wansdyke on Tan Hill which was shown on Andrews and Dury's 1773 map as 'St. Ann's Barn', and was illustrated on Colt Hoare's plate of Wansdyke in his *Ancient Wiltshire* (1819). This barn was probably used to store the many hurdles which would have been required for the fair.

Wansdyke on Tan Hill, looking west

South of Tan Hill, Clifford's Hill thrusts a headland south into the Vale to All Cannings Cross where an Iron Age settlement was excavated early this century. Clifford's Hill is crowned by two Neolithic earthworks, one of them a causewayed enclosure known as Rybury. The views from Tan Hill and Clifford's Hill are quite spectacular and are well worth a walk from Cannings Cross Farm, one mile south of Tan Hill fair site and half a mile south of Rybury, where a car can be conveniently parked.

East of Clifford's Hill a huge bowl-shaped coombe indented into Tan Hill is succeeded by Milk Hill which is carved with the Alton Barnes White Horse and has near its summit a dewpond called Oxenmere which is at least a thousand years old. Adam's Grave on Walker's Hill – which gets its name from Clement Walker who died in 1801 – is the most dramatically sited long barrow in Wiltshire, and possibly in Wessex. It is remarkable how prehistoric man consistently improved the landscape by his works: in this instance Adam's Grave positively enhances the appearance of Walker's Hill. Wansdyke runs a little to the north of all these hills and it was near Adam's Grave, which is situated a mile south of Red Shore, the strategic point where the Ridgeway crosses Wansdyke, that two major battles were fought in 592 and 715 AD at the time when Wessex was being taken over by the Anglo-Saxons. Between Walker's Hill and Knap Hill the Ridgeway crosses the col before plunging south to cross the Vale of Pewsey.

Walker's Hill, capped by Adam's Grave long barrow, seen from Knap Hill.

Approached from the north, this col provides one of the great experiences of Wiltshire downland. Proceeding south-west along the minor road from Lockeridge, as Wansdyke is crossed the smooth swell of Knap Hill appears to the left, with to the right Adam's Grave long barrow looming on Walker's Hill. There is little warning of the experience to come. As the gap between these hills is passed, the road begins to descend and the whole glorious spread of Pewsey Vale is suddenly revealed, together with an oblique view along the superb north escarpment of The Vale to Martinsell to the left. The experience must be similar to that recorded by Cobbett when he approached the Vale of Pewsey over Milton Hill on the opposite side in one of his 'Rural Rides' in August 1826, and sat enthralled on his horse for half an hour, although he 'had not breakfasted'!

Sometimes the steep slopes of the chalk downs are terraced into narrow steps merely a few inches wide and following the contours. An example is the lower east flank of Walker's Hill. Because they are often followed by sheep these steps have become known as 'sheep-paths', but it was not the tread of sheep which originally formed them. They result from solifluxion, which is the downward creep of topsoil as a result of alternate freezing and thawing, and of water action. Their proper name is terracettes.

Knap Hill is surmounted by a Neolithic causewayed camp. Such camps are now believed to have been prehistoric stock-holding enclosures. They are probably better referred to as causewayed enclosures, and the discovery of a Medieval hearth and the foundations of a small rectangular building constructed of chalk blocks on this hill, together with much pottery of seventeenth century date, suggests that a long tradition of stock-holding at Knap Hill may have continued until a comparatively recent date. I have often picked up fragments of clay pipes on Knap Hill, identified as made by Bristol manufacturers in the seventeenth century. These suggest that Knap Hill may have been a place of assembly for shepherds and drovers two miles east of Tan Hill fair site. This theory is supported by Mrs. Cunnington's excavation report which concluded that the kite-shaped enclosure added to the north-east side of the causewayed enclosure was Romano-British and that it had been: 'used as a fold or penning for flocks, chiefly perhaps for sheep, the inner enclosure affording additional protection for the weak and sickly ones, and perhaps a shelter for shepherds'.

Medieval traffic ways score the north-west shoulder of Knap Hill, and the Workway Drove running from Tan Hill and Wansdyke towards Pewsey cuts a deep groove over the south side of Knap Hill.

The Wiltshire writer Geoffrey Grigson used to relate an amusing anecdote connected with Knap Hill. The edible Roman snail is sometimes found on the calcareous soils of southern England, and Grigson was showing an American visitor the area and explaining its prehistory. The American, presumably lacking any conception of such distant history, was sceptical. Grigson pointed out the enclosure that had been added to Knap Hill and explained that it was Roman. 'And I suppose this is a Roman snail' said the New Yorker sarcastically. 'And it was! And it was!', exulted Grigson.

Immediately east of Knap Hill, Golden Ball Hill is believed to derive its name from the yellow rock rose – *Helianthemum vulgare* – which formerly covered this down and is still present on Knap Hill. On the north side of Golden Ball Hill stands Pit Pond (128 642), an old pond fringed with pines which would have been used by drovers moving their animals from Tan Hill fair site towards Marlborough.

The next hill is Draycot Hill with Gopher Wood, and on the spur overlooking Huish village are a number of tumuli (139 639). Several ditches exist at the north end of Gopher Wood suggesting considerable prehistoric activity on this hill. These earthworks immediately north-east of Gopher Wood are referred to as *boscus de Hulwerk* in the 1257 Savernake Forest charters. Less than a mile north is the site of the deserted downland village of Shaw which was abandoned early, probably in the fifteenth century.

Huish Hill and Oare Hill are covered with a multitude of prehistoric earthworks which, since they are cut into the south-facing escarpment, are best viewed from the Vale of Pewsey or from the Giant's Grave to their south-east.

The crowning glory of this range of hills stands at its east end. Martinsell is 'a presence and a personality' enthused H.W. Timperley in *The Vale of Pewsey* (1954), in which he devoted an entire chapter to this single hill. Timperley could not recall a single disappointing visit to Martinsell, and neither can I. 'It is one of those hills which takes possession of the imagination from the start' says Timperley, and all who walk in Wiltshire will appreciate his meaning, for the great bastion of this hill dominates Pewsey Vale and is a landmark for half the county. Martinsell is distantly visible from Shrewton on Salisbury Plain, from near Westbury in west Wiltshire, and from the nearer Marlborough Downs its presence is nearly always felt. Its distinctive profile crowned by its ragged trees is visible from for example Round Hill Downs near Aldbourne, from most of the

Ridgeway in Wiltshire, from Fyfield Down and Hackpen, and from the northern hillforts of Barbury and Liddington, eight and nine miles distant. Massingham wrote: 'Never did hill throw out so bold and soaring a bluff as Martinsell over the valley', and Dean Farrar when head of Marlborough School wrote of 'the natural amphitheatre of Martinsell, and the glorious expanse on which I had gazed so often from its green and breezy summit'.

In the eighteenth century there was a summer house on The Giant's Grave promontory which reaches west from Martinsell, and in 1806 the archaeologist Colt Hoare wrote in a letter: 'From the Summer House observe the finest view in Wiltshire'. The views from Martinsell certainly are spectacular and take in most of the landmarks of north Wiltshire.

Every one who knows the hill seems to come under the spell of Martinsell, one of the most recent being Anthony Blunt who went to Cambridge and from the 1930s spied for the Russians at the time when they were opposed to Hitler. He must have known Martinsell from being at Marlborough College, and loved it well enough to direct that his ashes were to be scattered on the hill.

The top of the track which rises from Oare Hill around Rainscombe to Martinsell was known as Ravensgate (169 641). Rainscombe is believed to get its name from *hraefnes cumb* meaning raven's valley, suggesting that this may have been a haunt of ravens. Buzzards still (1991) nest at Ravensgate.

Fairs used to be held on Martinsell but were discontinued in 1860, and on Palm Sunday everyone in Wootton Rivers used to visit it for hillside sports. The shepherd's cottage which stood near the derelict barn on the summit (at 173 636) west of the hillfort was said to be the highest inhabited dwelling in Wiltshire. The last resident – Harry Pinchin I believe – considered Martinsell to be 'as healthy a place to live as you could wish'. In *Household Words* (1867) Charles Dickens published 'The Ghost of Pit Pond', which is the pond below the church in Huish village. In the story he has the shepherd on Martinsell saying:

> They do say them that's out at sea, mariners and suchlike, can see the very place we're standin' on; leastways the white house yon, top of Martin's Hill where the soldiers' graves are. What soldiers I asked? He couldn't tell. [see page 150 for the possible source of this story].

Western Escarpment

At the west edge of the Marlborough Downs a double escarpment cuts first through the Lower Chalk and then through the Upper Chalk. The flat shelf of land between the escarpments is about three miles wide near Broad Hinton but widens to about six miles near Avebury. This shelf carries the A4361 Devizes to Swindon road which provides the west boundary of the Marlborough Downs for the purposes of this book; the lower escarpment west of the road is therefore excluded, but the higher escarpment hills are within our area. These carry the Ridgeway along their crest from Overton Hill to Barbury Castle.

Overton Hill has a Bronze Age barrow cemetery with Romano-British graves added to it, and secondary Saxon interments inserted into some of the barrows. This hill was almost certainly the site of the battle in 1006 when the Anglo-Saxon levies mustered at East Kennett half a mile south of Overton Hill to intercept a Viking raiding party taking their booty towards the south coast (see later page 64). Following the Ridgeway north

Beech clumps on Avebury Down from the south-west. Some of the clumps are placed on round barrows.

from Overton Hill we are soon on Avebury Down. To the left Avebury village is embowered in trees, and on the ridge to the east may be seen the experimental earthwork which was constructed in 1960. Beyond this earthwork and behind the brow of the hill are the sarsen stones and the archaeological riches of Overton Down and Fyfield Down.

The track which the Ridgeway crosses (at 125 708) a mile and a half east of Avebury was formerly the main coach road between London and Bristol by way of Marlborough and Avebury. The down between Avebury and the Ridgeway is punctuated with a number of beech clumps, some of which have been planted on round barrows.

Continuing northwards we are soon on the south end of Hackpen Hill with Glory Ann a little to the east, and Monkton Down thrusting out towards Winterbourne Monkton to the west. This down is studded with tumuli and a probable long barrow, and may well be an unrecognised settlement site. The long arc of Hackpen has earthworks, tumuli, sarsen stones, and an inferior White Horse opposite Broad Hinton. The 'pen' in Hackpen is one of the few Wiltshire examples of the old Celtic word for a hill, and the 'hack' may be from the Old English 'haca' meaning hook. Hackpen Hill is embellished with three distinctive beech clumps which must be eighteenth or early-nineteenth century decorative plantings and are a considerable landmark. The thorns on Hackpen are encrusted with lichens which are a testament to the purity of the air on this almost 274 metres height which rises some 91 metres from the road below.

Travelling the minor road between Marlborough and Broad Hinton past Rockley is an experience that should not be missed. The road undulates delightfully over Rough Down, then after passing Old Eagle near Rockley it runs along a wooded coombe past Rockley Firs. It then re-enters open downland with wide views as it rises to Hackpen Hill where it crosses the Ridgeway and then plunges down a winding descent past the Hackpen White Horse to the plain which occupies a shelf between the upper and lower escarpments at the west edge of the Marlborough Downs.

Hackpen forms the dividing line between the high downland sheepwalks to its south-east and the low clay plains to its north-west where cattle husbandry predominated, and it is said to have been here that the old Wiltshire expression 'as different as chalk from cheese' originated.

Barbury and Liddington

At the north-east end of Hackpen Hill the Ridgeway dips from a height of almost 274 metres to about 229 metres as it crosses a minor road from Wroughton. The old Ridgeway here runs on north-east across the lower ground, but the Countryside Commission's Ridgeway climbs the west end of Barbury hillfort to resume a height of almost 274 metres on Barbury Castle. In this dip on Uffcott Down a Romano-British burial was found when an oil pipeline was dug in 1985. As the descent from Hackpen begins, Faringdon Clump is visible on the distant horizon ahead, and Liddington Hill and its tree clump may be seen beyond Barbury. To the right and two miles away is Four Mile Clump, and further round is the ragged crest of Martinsell at a distance of about ten miles on the horizon at the southern edge of the Marlborough Downs.

Hackpen Hill beech clumps from Barbury Castle ramparts.

Barbury Castle commands – as does Liddington Castle opposite – the head of the valley of the River Og which provided one of the principal approaches into Wessex from the north. It was here at Barbury that in 556 was fought the Battle of *Beranburh* as the Saxons from the Upper Thames Valley pushed south into Wiltshire. The old Ordnance Survey marked 'Beranburh 556' in gothic lettering with crossed swords (at 147 769) immediately west of the little copse which is overlooked from the north ramparts of Barbury Castle. I do not know if there was any authority for locating the battle at this precise point; it seems unlikely, and I note that it is omitted from the recent Pathfinder map. Another but less direct military matter connected with Barbury is the fact that the great general John Churchill, who was created Duke of Marlborough as a reward for his victories over the French early in the eighteenth century, bought the manor of Barbury in 1709 and it remained in the family until 1877.

The archaeology of the magnificent hillfort of Barbury is described elsewhere. It, together with Liddington, was frequented by Richard Jefferies and Alfred Williams who were in 1939 commemorated by the erection of a sarsen stone dedicated to them on Burderop Down, a little east of Barbury Castle Country Park car park.

Very occasionally when walking in downland you may find a secluded little coombe hedged in on all sides by gently sloping downs which block the views in all directions. The attraction of such places is that in them, in this practically treeless landscape, you are alone with down and sky. Here you experience the true spirit of the Downs. A similar experience on a smaller scale may be obtained by descending into the fosse of a hillfort. These secret coombes are often too unimportant to warrant even a name. They are frequently crossed by little-used footpaths, and are one of the delights of the Downs. I was recently in such a coombe a little south of Barbury Castle and found myself in the company of four fallow deer who were so unused to human intruders in their little-frequented fastness that they did not run away but stood and stared in curious disbelief. It is my experience that if you continue to walk when you chance unexpectedly upon wild deer they will sometimes stand their ground and accept your presence. On this occasion, having a feeling that I had intruded upon privacy, I walked slowly out of the coombe and left its occupants to resume their enjoyment of their remote sanctuary. Continuing east from Barbury, towards the east end of Smeathe's Ridge a little elevated knoll (176 753) attains over 213 metres. It is a fine perch for a picnic lunch or for a drink halt on a walk because it commands a breathtaking view of the Marlborough Downs from Liddington Hill in the north-east to Martinsell seven miles distant on the southern horizon, with Four Mile Clump three quarters of a mile away to the south-west. In the foreground the round island of Smeathe's Plantation stands in winter in a dark brown expanse of ploughland, in summer in a sea of waving corn.

South of Smeathe's Ridge on the turnpike road from Swindon to Marlborough stands Four Mile Clump which obtains its name from being four miles from Marlborough. This favourite place of the poet Charles Sorley was probably a halting place for drovers following the turnpike to the fairs at Marlborough because on its north edge is a pond. The clump was not shown on Andrews and Dury in 1773 but it appears on the first Ordnance Survey which came out fifty years later.

From Barbury Castle the true Ridgeway – as opposed to the Ridgeway Long Distance Trail – crosses the Og Valley and the former Burderop Racecourse as it runs north-east to Liddington Hill which is topped by an Iron Age hill fort and may possibly have been the site of the Battle of Badon. It is situated between the true but now-metalled prehistoric Ridgeway to its north, and the line adopted for the Countryside Commission's Long Distance Trail to its south-east. Liddington is justly celebrated as the hill where the young Richard Jefferies experienced the feelings which later in his life he wrote into his remarkable biography *The Story of My Heart*:

> There was a hill to which I used to resort at such periods....Moving up the sweet short turf, at every step my heart seemed to obtain a wider horizon of feeling....By the time I had reached the summit I had entirely forgotten the petty circumstances and annoyances of existence. I felt myself, myself. There was an intrenchment on the summit, and going down into the fosse I walked round it slowly to recover breath. On the south-western side there was a spot where the bank had partially slipped, leaving a gap. There the view was over a broad plain, beautiful with wheat, and inclosed by a perfect amphitheatre of green hills. Through these hills there was a narrow groove, or pass, southwards, where the white clouds seemed to close in the horizon. Woods hid the scattered hamlets and farmhouses, so that I was quite alone.

I have quoted Jefferies at some length because Liddington Hill is inevitably linked with *The Story of My Heart*, written in 1883 by a thirty-five year-old invalid four years from an early death, exiled from his beloved Marlborough Downs and unappreciated in his own time, pouring into his book the thoughts which he had experienced on Liddington as a youth seventeen years before. There seems to be no middle course with *The Story of My Heart*; it positively repels or attracts its readers. Jefferies tells us that he had been 'meditating seventeen years' over the book which he described as his 'autobiographical confessions' and as 'absolutely and unflinchingly true'. When asked by his publisher C.J. Longman to provide an analysis of his book Jefferies found himself at a loss and in a letter confessed 'I find it impossible to do so'.

Liddington Hill and Clump (left) from the west

No one wishing to visit Liddington Hill should be deterred by the apparent lack of footpaths on to the hill. A 'permissive' path runs, by agreement with the landowner, from the tree clump at the east end of Liddington along the fence line on to the hillfort, and the path can easily be reached along another fence line running north from a point (213 797) on the Ridgeway Long Distance Trail. On the hillfort the steps of Jefferies may be followed round the fosse to the point at the south-west corner 'where the outer bank had partially slipped'. Here the view enjoyed by Richard Jefferies may be seen little altered since his time despite the intervening 130 years, over the 'broad plain' and though the 'narrow groove, or gap' of the Og Valley into the heart of the Marlborough Downs. In the foreground of that view below the west end of Liddington Hill is Liddington Folly, a windswept clump of trees. At the opposite and east end of the hill stands Liddington Clump, a similarly wind-harassed clump of trees that is visible far into Berkshire, now Oxfordshire.

The villagers of Liddington used to create amusement by announcing that they were 'off to dig for a pig' on Liddington Hill. By this they meant that they intended to exercise their right to dig for flints which they sold to the local surveyor for road-making. They then used the proceeds to buy the cottage pig which they fattened to furnish them with bacon, chitterlings, sweetbreads, trotters and pig's head with which they augmented their meagre and otherwise meat-free diet.

A little south of Liddington the Upham Ridge runs east from above Lower Upham with a dip into a dry coombe-head a little west of Upper Upham. On this ridge, at an altitude of about 250 metres, Upper Upham provides an example of a site occupied practically continuously from prehistoric through Roman and Medieval to modern times.

Sugar Hill is the long smooth ridge of downland which runs south-east from near Liddington Hill for about four miles to Aldbourne. It is, in the words of H.W. Timperley, 'one of the pleasures of the north Wiltshire Downs', and the views from it over the motorway to the north-east are more than compensated by the view across Shipley Bottom to Upper Upham and its field systems on the opposite ridge. The area south-west of Sugar Hill was formerly devoted to rabbit-warrening, but the Liddington and Aldbourne Warrens were ploughed during the Napoleonic Wars to grow wheat and the warrens are today commemorated only by the two farms which bear their names. Sugar Hill is crowned by a number of prehistoric remains, the most obvious being the superbly sited Four Barrows, burial mounds of W.H. Hudson's 'long, dead, who knew not life in towns, and felt no strangeness in sun, wind and rain'.

Shipley Bottom, west of Sugar Hill, is another example of the enclosed coombes of the Marlborough Downs, described by Edward Thomas:

> ..then through Shipley Bottom, where stands a barn and stacks under ash and sycamore and elder, in the midst of corn, and walled on every side by down and sky. There the painted lady butterfly comes to the scabious flower and the bee to the sweet basil in perfect solitude.

Shipley Bottom Barn – which was 'Warren Barn' on Andrews and Dury in 1773 when the rabbit warren still existed, but was 'Shipley Bottom Barn' on the first Ordnance Survey – is now gone (it stood at 222 782) but its trees survive. One of my most abiding memories of the landscape of the Marlborough Downs is the sight of Sugar Hill momentarily illuminated by the rosy glow of the setting sun as I walked east along Shipley Bottom at the end of a long overcast day spent walking on the Downs. That memorable moment more than made up for the dull weather of the rest of the day.

My descriptions of the hills of the Marlborough Downs ends with Sugar Hill. Reflecting on these hills, the best are Barbury, Liddington, Sugar Hill and Martinsell. Barbury is magnificent, and Liddington evokes Richard Jefferies, but both are marred by the proximity of Swindon, and Liddington also by the motorway. Timperley wrote of Sugar Hill: 'As long as I can find such places at home I want no peaks on the distant roof of the world', but for me Martinsell at the remote southern edge of the Marlborough Downs is supreme.

Devil's Den in Clatford Bottom

3 Prehistoric Legacy

The feature of the Marlborough Downs which most closely rivals the attraction of their topography and hills is the archaeological remains, those survivals from the distant unwritten past. These downlands were the abode of early man prior to the wooded valleys becoming more readily accessible to him, and in the Marlborough Downs are to be found the greatest concentration of archaeological field monuments in Britain.

The archaeologist Peter Fowler, referring to the profusion of often unexplained archaeological remains which are concentrated in this district and make it an ideal area for 'reading' the landscape and speculating about its past, has described the Avebury area and the Marlborough Downs as 'a great archive' and as 'a library of many "books" embedded in the landscape'.

NEOLITHIC (from about 4,000 BC to 2,400 BC)

The Neolithic or New Stone Age derives its name from the fact that its people made extensive use of stone prior to the discovery of metals. The archaeological field monuments of this period in the Marlborough Downs are many and varied. Extensive use was made of the indigenous sarsen stones in arrangements of standing stones and for the portals and chambers of long barrows. Neolithic man also constructed causewayed enclosures for purposes which are not yet understood. They seem to have been sites where men and animals congregated, and since their function has not been established I prefer the term 'enclosure' – which they were – rather than the more usual term causewayed 'camp', which they may not have been. It is possible that they were the predecessors of the ritual henge monuments such as Avebury and Stonehenge.

This area is so very rich in archaeological remains that I shall not enter into long descriptions of the better-known field monuments which have been perfectly well described elsewhere. In the account of prehistory which follows I shall restrict descriptions to the minor field monuments, and to some aspects of the more famous monuments which may have been neglected, for it is not necessarily the best known sites that stir the imagination. Often it is the remoter less-frequented sites which can be enjoyed in solitude because few people visit them.

Avebury

Avebury Henge Monument – 'henge' comes from a Saxon word meaning hanging, and refers to the lintels or hanging stones of Stonehenge – is an embanked stone circle constructed at the end of the Neolithic period presumably as a religious or ceremonial monument since the ditch is inside the bank. It encircles part of Avebury village which was in part constructed out of its demolished standing stones. The removal of these stones was encouraged by the church which in the Middle Ages regarded the pagan monument as a competitor which was best eliminated. Although Stonehenge was well known, Avebury was not recognised until John Aubrey discovered and promoted it in the seventeenth century. By the early twentieth century Avebury had been reduced to a sorry state, but the stones which survived were saved and others re-erected (some had been buried) by the Scottish millionaire Alexander Keiller in the 1930s, but his work was interrupted by the war.

A particular point about Avebury henge monument should be emphasised. A popular misconception has arisen that Avebury and Stonehenge were created by the Druids as ceremonial centres, and in 1773 Andrews and Dury's map of Wiltshire marks Avebury as 'Supposed by Antiquarians to be a Druid's Temple'. The Druids were a Celtic priesthood who were active in the Iron Age from about 300 BC. They were suppressed by the Romans in both Gaul and Britain. Avebury and Stonehenge originated in the Neolithic period and predated the Druidic cult by about 2,000 years. Druidism was essentially pre-Christian and as the pagan Celtic world was not literate the little knowledge we have of the Druids comes from Classical sources. Much of what is imagined to be Druidic derives from the wildly romantic imaginings of seventeenth and eighteenth century antiquaries such as John Aubrey and William Stukeley. Their theories are accepted only by the credulous, but a cult of fanciful

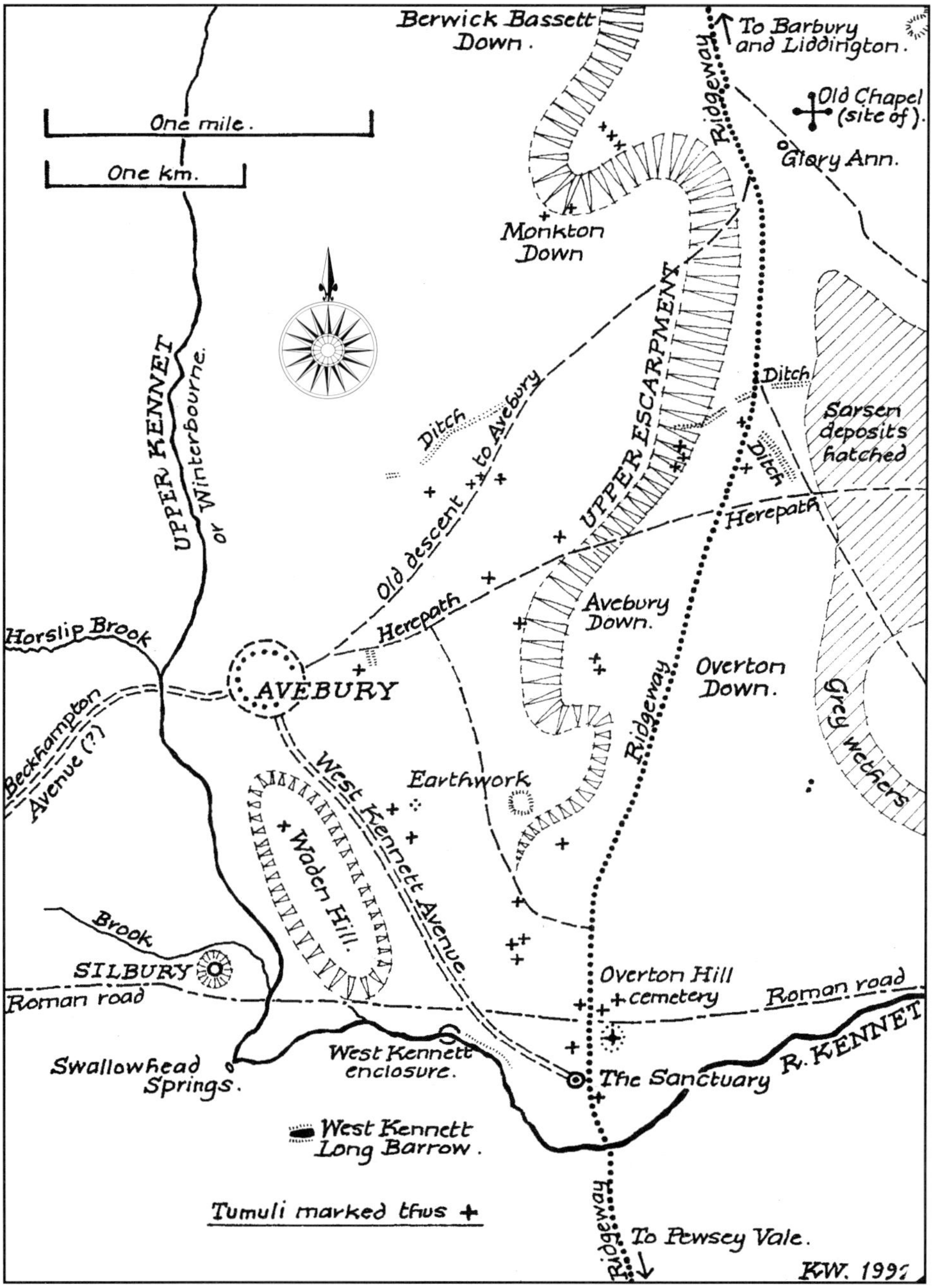

The Avebury district in prehistoric times

Druidism has been created in modern times. The association of the Druids with any prehistoric site is an assumption which has not been proved, although this does not preclude the possibility that they may have adopted existing centres such as Avebury for their ceremonial.

Causewayed Enclosures

Slightly more than a mile north-west of Avebury and strictly outside the limits of the Marlborough Downs as defined for the purposes of this book is the little-frequented causewayed enclosure of Windmill Hill. It was this Neolithic site which brought Alexander Keiller to this area on a rescue operation when a wireless company proposed to erect a number of radio masts on the hill. The scheme was dropped but Keiller bought Windmill Hill to secure its future, excavated it, and then proceeded to do the same for nearby Avebury. The other major causewayed enclosure – so-called from the original causeways which cross the ditches – in the area is Knap Hill on the scarp overlooking the Vale of Pewsey. This was the first causewayed enclosure to be excavated, by Mr. and Mrs. Cunnington in 1908-9. Rybury, on Clifford's Hill, is a minor causewayed enclosure.

Silbury Hill

Closely associated with Avebury is Silbury Hill, the mysterious conical man-made mound which is so immense that it has been designated 'hill', which is unusual for a man-made construction. Silbury is undoubtedly Neolithic although its purpose has never been established. Sometimes it has been described as a barrow, but many tunnelled explorations at various times have failed to discover a primary burial, although Stukeley recorded a possible Saxon burial near the top in 1723. The barrow theory also ignores the fact that Silbury long predates round barrows, the barrows of the Neolithic period being invariably long barrows. The 'bury' element in the name of Silbury is of interest. It may derive from the Old English 'beorg' meaning barrow, but if it is from the Old English 'byrig' this suggests that the Saxons at least regarded Silbury as a defensive work, and we know that they fortified it in 1010 when the Viking hosts were marauding in this area.

Knap Hill causewayed enclosure from the Workway Drove to its north-east.

An interesting aspect of Silbury which seems never to have been noticed is that ever since it was first illustrated by Aubrey in the seventeenth century all the drawings of Silbury confirm that the path to its summit which winds round the west flank of the hill has remained unaltered. This is therefore presumably the route by which Charles II and James II – then Duke of York – were conducted by Aubrey up the hill. But an even more interesting fact is that all the early illustrators of Silbury Hill, including Aubrey, Stukeley, and Colt Hoare's illustrator Philip Crocker, have drawm Silbury far steeper than it actually is. The drawing made by the Rev. A.C.Smith in 1859 to record the visit of the Wiltshire Archaeological Society to Silbury similarly grossly exaggerated the slope of the mound, representing it as more than forty-five degrees, and even A.D.Passmore in the 1920s (in his sketch in Avebury Museum) made the same mistake. Not the least intriguing mystery about Silbury is the way in which it has exercised a peculiar compulsion upon its illustrators to exaggerate the slope of its mound.

Silbury Hill from the upper Kennet Winterbourne to its east.

Long Barrows

Long barrows are long earthen mounds constructed for multiple burials. Some had stone chambers incorporated in them. They are represented in the Marlborough Downs by West Kennett Barrow, the best known long barrow with multiple stone chambers which may be entered to a depth of some fourteen metres, the larger but unexcavated East Kennett Barrow which is covered with trees and has no right-of-way to it, Adam's Grave on Walker's Hill which is the most dramatically sited long barrow in Wiltshire, and the Devil's Den a little north of the A4 in Clatford Bottom. This is the surviving stone chamber of an earthen long barrow from which the earth has at some time been removed. It is unusually sited in a valley bottom, and its stones were in fact re-erected in 1921.

Another Neolithic long barrow which has now entirely disappeared was associated with what seems to have been a mortuary enclosure beside the Ridgeway at Glory Ann on the south end of Hackpen Hill. The old Ordnance Survey marked 'Long Barrow (Site of)' at 129 729 and we only know about this site from the writings of William Stukeley who described and sketched it in 1723. He called the structure which he saw 'Old Chapel'

West Kennett Long Barrow blocking stones from the north-east

and described it in Abury Described (1743):

> Tis a large square, entrenched, 110 druid cubits by 130 (that is 48 yards by 57 yards)....with one entrance on the southwest towards Abury. The enclosure is made of a vallum and ditch; beyond that a row of flat stones set quite round and pretty close to one another like a wall.

Stukeley also saw a long barrow with its entrance abutting the north-east side of the enclosure, the barrow being similarly set round with stones. He also mentions 'a great cavity call'd Balmore pond....It answers exactly to the Old Chapel entrance'. We cannot be sure whether this was the present Glory Ann pond, but this pond is set with sarsen stones and was formerly known as Belmont pond.

A hundred years after Stukeley, in 1821, Colt Hoare came in search of 'Old Chapel'. In *Ancient Wiltshire* he wrote:

> From hence, I ascended a hill to the N.W. directing my course

towards a cottage adjoining the trackway distinguished by the fanciful title of Glory Ann, leaving the vale in which Wick Farm is situated on my right . To the North East of Glory Ann, I, with some difficulty, discovered the antiquities mentioned by Stukeley under the name of Old Chapel, a large square entrenched.

It is evident from Stukeley's description and drawings that in Old Chapel there existed a major Neolithic monument which Colt Hoare experienced 'some difficulty' in finding nearly two hundred years ago. Now it is entirely gone and the field in which it stood is regularly ploughed.

Standing Stones

Arrangements of standing stones, in for example circles or avenues, normally belong to the Neolithic period. An example of an avenue is the West Kennett Avenue which ran in a slightly serpentine line south-east from Avebury for about a mile and a half to The Sanctuary on Overton Hill. This double row of standing stones, much of which survives, has alternating columnar and flat sarsens which may represent male and female figures. Presumably it was a processional way. It has always been assumed that prehistoric men moved large sarsen stones with timber rollers, but in an address to the Wiltshire Archaeological Society in 1894 Mr. Joshua Brooke suggested that the many spherical sarsen stones, too large for pot boilers or sling-stones, which he had found in the Avebury area, might have been used as rollers.

The Sanctuary stands at the southern end of West Kennett Avenue immediately south of the A4 beside the lay-by on Overton Hill. I mention this fact because it was incorrectly plotted by the Ordnance Survey further south on their Pathfinder map, but the position is obvious on site. The Sanctuary, which was lost but rediscovered in the present century by Mrs. Cunnington, consisted of a series of concentric stone circles of undoubted Neolithic date with probably a circular timber building at the centre. It is likely to have been used for funerary ritual and exposure of corpses prior to interment at West Kennett Barrow which stands half a mile west of its site. Another arrangement of standing stones in a circle was recorded by John Aubrey at Clatford but is now gone without trace. It was known as 'Broadstone Ring'. West of Avebury two standing stones known as the

Standing stone on Overton Down a little west of Delling Copse, probably erected as a rubbing post for cattle

Longstones or Adam and Eve (089 693) have been re-erected where they were discovered. These may be survivals of the Beckhampton Avenue mentioned by Stukeley as running west from Avebury, the rest of which may – if it ever existed – have been destroyed when an Anglo-Saxon settlement was established west of Avebury.

Single standing stones, known as monoliths or menhirs, present a particular problem with regard to dating. Some may be Neolithic but generally they are undatable. O.G.S. Crawford suggested in *Archaeology in the Field* (1953) that the question: What are standing stones? was unanswerable, and that their purpose was uncertain. Isolated standing stones are sometimes found in the Marlborough Downs and may be prehistoric or later. Single stones may have been erected as scratching posts for cattle, and this is probably the case with the example west of Delling Copse on Overton Down (129 712). One sarsen was erected as late as 1939 on Burderop Down as a memorial to Richard Jefferies and Alfred Williams, which indicates the long span of time over which standing stones were erected. Several occur on Fyfield Down, a good example being the stone known as Long Tom (144 713). This is a narrow columnar sarsen about two and a half metres high. Its situation on a parish boundary suggests, assuming that the boundary predates the stone, a late Saxon or early Medieval date for the stone. Alternatively it may have been erected to mark a way over the Downs, for it stands on the line of the road from Totterdown to Clatford designated a second-class road by Britton in 1809, in which case it may be late-Medieval or post-Medieval. Two standing stones may be seen embedded in a hedgerow a little south-west of Down Barn (at 129 695) east of the Ridgeway, on a footpath three quarters of a mile north of the A4.

The mystery arising from not knowing the purpose or the time of origin of standing stones is often emphasised by the remoteness of their setting, although the artist Paul Nash described even the standing stones of the Avebury stone circle in their village setting as 'wonderful and disquieting'.

The discovery in the late 1980s of a major archaeological site on the river at West Kennett Farm (109 682) a little over a mile from Avebury and between the West Kennett Barrow and The Sanctuary is of great interest in view of the lack of a known prehistoric settlement site associated with Avebury. Excavation may prove the site at West Kennett Farm to be the dwelling place of the people who created Avebury and its associated Neolithic monuments.

One of the lesser known and little visited Neolithic elements in the Marlborough Downs is the polissoir on Overton Down. The fact that it is practically unknown is probably due to three reasons: it has never been marked on the Ordnance Survey, it was missed in the *Victoria County History* archaeological gazeteer, and it is on private ground about seventy-three metres east of the Ridgeway (at 128 715). The polissoir is one of two examples in England of a Neolithic axe grinding and polishing bench although more examples exist in France, polissoir being of course French for polisher. This sarsen has five grooves in its top face for sharpening edges of cutting tools, and a saucer-shaped cuvette for polishing the faces of the stone axes which were probably used to fell trees to provide rollers to move sarsens. The polissoir has been split at its north-west corner by sarsen masons, and the marks of two splitting wedges may be seen at the top of the split, but for some reason it was then left undisturbed.

The sarsen stone known as the polissoir on Overton Down near Delling Copse

BRONZE AGE (from about 2400 BC to 700 BC)

Round Barrows

Although the later phases of activity at Avebury are attributable to the Bronze Age, Avebury temple is essentially Neolithic. The principal visible evidence of the Bronze Age in the Marlborough Downs is provided by the round barrows which are plentiful in the area and are marked on the map as 'tumuli' or in the singular 'tumulus'.

These round barrows, which are burial mounds, are almost invariably of the Bronze Age although Iron Age, Roman and Saxon examples are known. They are of various types with sometimes variations between types, and the proportions have been established for Wessex as 87% bowl, 6% bell, 4% disc, 2% saucer and 1% pond. It will be seen that the great preponderance of barrows is of the simple bowl type resembling an inverted basin.

Richard Jefferies felt an affinity with the people buried in the barrows when he wrote:

> There were grass grown tumuli on the hills to which of old I used to walk, sit down at the foot of one of them, and think. Some warrior had been interred there in the ante-historic times. The sun of the summer morning shone on the dome of the sward, and....I felt at that moment that I was like the spirit of the man whose body was interred in the tumulus.

Round barrows vary considerably in size. They occur in isolation, in groups and sometimes in alignments. The latter is often seen on Salisbury Plain but is less common in the Marlborough Downs. Perhaps the best-sited group of round barrows in this area is Four Barrows on the ridge of Sugar Hill one and a half miles north-west of Aldbourne where three bell barrows and one bowl are aligned along the track which follows the crest of the hill. A readily accessible and more random group of round barrows may be seen in the barrow cemetery on Overton Hill where the Ridgeway crosses the A4. These were recorded as *Seofon-beorges* (Seven Barrows) in the tenth century AD, and some of these barrows have secondary Saxon interments. Bronze Age round barrows are normally sited on ridges, or in positions on slopes where they were silhouetted when seen from below. The latter siting seems to imply use by the Bronze Age people of the lower ground, although barrows were not normally sited in valley bottoms except very occasionally near rivers and springs, as at Rockley.

At Ogbourne St. Andrew there exists an unusual occurrence in the existence of a Bronze Age tumulus in the churchyard. The local people availed themselves of its existence in such a convenient position to insert about twenty secondary burials into this pagan barrow in consecrated ground. Barrows often line old traffic routes, as in the Sugar Hill case noted above. Another example is the succession of tumuli including a very fine pond barrow (167 764) which occur at intervals along the ridge track which becomes Gipsy Lane as it runs east from Barbury over Burderop Down towards the Aldbourne area. Many other barrows are to be found in the Marlborough Downs although a great many were ploughed down during the twentieth century before steps were taken to protect them.

Linear earthworks

Within the Marlborough Downs there is a multitude of unexplained linear earthworks, for example the long range running south from Liddingon Hill over Whitefield Hill along the east escarpment of the Og Valley, the many linear banks on Overton and Fyfield Downs, and the earthwork which runs through Yielding Copse (221 734). These linear earthworks, like standing stones, present a problem with regard to dating, and it is difficult to interpret their functions. It is likely that some date from the Bronze Age, as well as from later prehistoric periods. Others may be Saxon or Medieval. A number of Bronze Age enclosures formerly existed on Ogbourne Down south of Smeathe's Ridge, but despite being regarded as the best group of late Bronze Age enclosures in Wessex they have now been ploughed down.

IRON AGE (from about 700 BC to 43 AD)

Hillforts

The most visible of our prehistoric monuments are the hillforts of the Iron Age which crown many hills. There are three of these in the Marlborough Downs. Barbury Castle and Liddington stand on the Ridgeway and controlled the valley of the Og which provided the principal pass from the north into the area which became Wessex, the land of the West Saxons. The third hillfort crowns Martinsell Hill at the southern edge of Marlborough Downs.

Liddington hillfort (left) seen from the north ramparts of Barbury Castle.

Barbury Castle is a remarkably strong bivallate (double-banked) example with sarsens built into its ramparts. The fort is oval in plan and encloses about eleven acres, the ramparts being about half a mile round. Aerial photographs have revealed hut circles inside the fort, which has to its east extensive field systems of probably Iron Age date on Burderop Down. The hillfort has been desecrated by a track which has been driven east to west through the middle of it. Near Barbury Castle the Battle of *Beranburh* was fought in AD 556. Opposite Barbury on the east side of the Og Valley is Liddington Castle. This hillfort was formerly known as both Battlesbury and Badbury Camp, which prompts the suggestion that perhaps the Battle of Mount Badon was fought here. In plan the north-west, north-east and south-east ramparts of Liddington form a square with rounded corners, while the south-west side is roughly semi-circular. The ramparts are univallate (single-banked) with a slight counterscarp and have slipped on the south-west side. The only original entrance seems to be on the south-east side. In common with most hillforts, Liddington remains unexcavated.

The third hillfort of the Marlborough Downs is Martinsell which is univallate, roughly rectangular in shape, and encloses thirty-two acres. Its only entrance seems to have been at its north-east corner. Outside this entrance on the east slope of Martinsell are a number of depressions (179 643) which have been the subject of much speculation among archaeologists. The Ordnance Survey formerly labelled them pit dwellings but later – at I believe the instigation of O.G.S. Crawford – this designation was withdrawn and today these pits are generally regarded as chalk diggings rather than the pit dwellings of an outguard. The ramparts of Martinsell are not as formidable as those of many hillforts, and the Martinsell enclosure is regarded by some as more of a cattle-enclosure associated with a settlement than as a hillfort.

From the south-west end of the Martinsell plateau runs a promontory called The Giant's Grave. This is a small Iron Age promontory fort of only two and a half acres. It is on a very steep and narrow spur and its only man-made defences are two slight ditches across the neck of the spur, with a strong bank and ditch west of them penetrated by an entrance. Much early Iron Age pottery has been picked up on The Giant's Grave and later Iron Age pottery just west of Martinsell hillfort, which suggests that the hillfort may have replaced the promontory fort when more space was needed.

It is the nature of Iron Age hillforts to occupy strong positions on the tops of hills which offered early warning of the approach of an enemy. Consequently the views from hillforts are invariably wide and well worth seeing, which in the case of the three Marlborough Downs hillforts requires little effort as all three are approached to within half a mile by a road.

Field Systems

At Fyfield Down two and a half miles east of Avebury exists an archaeological site with many periods represented which was described by Professor Fowler who excavated it as 'a better preserved area of earthworks than any other in Wessex'. Fyfield Down is included under the Iron Age because its Celtic field systems were in active use in that period although there seems to have been practically constant land use here throughout prehistory and into historic times. In the Neolithic period its sarsens were used to construct Avebury and the chambers and portals of long barrows. Subsequently settlement seems to have extended through the Bronze and Iron Age field systems to its exploitation during the Romano-British period. In the late Romano-British period there is evidence that much of the arable was abandoned to pasture. This pasture probably continued into Anglo-Saxon times as there is evidence of fourth, fifth and tenth century settlements on Fyfield Down, followed by a twelfth and thirteenth century settlement south of Wroughton Copse, and a seventeenth century farm south of Delling Copse. It seems that in Fyfield Down we have an unusual example of a downland area in almost continuous occupation from the Neolithic period of prehistory to the seventeenth century.

The Celtic fields of Fyfield Down survive as lynchet banks at the edge of the prehistoric fields. Pottery in these lynchets suggest continuing use into the Iron Age.

Celtic field systems were formed when ploughing took place on a slope. Topsoil was displaced down the slope as a result of the disturbance, together with rainwash. At the top of the field the displacement left a step in the hillside known as a negative lynchet, and at the bottom – where ploughing stopped – the build-up of soil created a positive lynchet. Where one field is found abutting and below another the negative and positive lynchets combine to form a composite lynchet. Where boulders have been cleared to the edges of fields to allow uninterrupted ploughing these boulders contributed to the formation of very large lynchets by revetting the topsoil into field banks. It is the presence of large sarsen boulders in the banks which explains the scale of the Celtic field banks on Fyfield Down, some of which are over three metres high. Celtic fields tended to be rather square in shape and it is this fact which explains the occurrence of large banks on shallow slopes. Later lynchets tended to be narrower and followed the contours, and consequently are known as strip lynchets.

On Fyfield Down there are many ditches which are probably Bronze Age in origin, originally six feet deep and revetted with sarsen stones. These ditches later came to be used as trackways between the fields, and by the Roman period they had silted up to general ground level and were used as roadways probably by wheeled traffic. Those who wish to know more about Fyfield Down should refer to the extensive well illustrated interim excavation reports by Professor Fowler in *WAM 58* for December 1962 and September 1963.

More Iron Age systems which are to be found east of Barbury on Burderop Down (164 766) have already been mentioned.

ROMANO-BRITISH (from 43 AD to the early 5th century)

With the Romano-British period we arrive at a period of transition between prehistory and recorded history. The civilisation of Roman Britain was neither Roman nor British, it was Romano-British with the Romanised Britons continuing the activities which they had practised in the Iron Age through the *Pax Romana* but under the control of Roman overlords. The essentially Iron Age framework of rural settlement and agriculture survived practically intact as the Romans left the existing farming system virtually undisturbed; evidence indicates that probably ninety per cent of the Iron Age field systems of Wessex continued to be used during the Romano-British period. The system was probably improved and certainly exploited, for Professor Hawkes demonstrated that the increased production of corn during the Romano-British period was offset by the demands of the Roman authorities and that probably more than half the corn production was appropriated to feed the army or for export.

The impact of Roman methods and organisation on the established agricultural systems of the Iron Age is one of the most interesting aspects of the Romano-British countryside.

The principal Roman contributions to the landscape were their towns and roads, but there are no Roman towns within the area I have defined as the Marlborough Downs. The few Roman roads will be discussed later under communications.

Despite the fact that Roman stations existed at the perimeter of the Marlborough Downs at Wanborough (*Durocornovium*), east of Marlborough (*Cunetio*) and at Sandy Lane near Calne (*Verlucio*), the Roman period is not well represented in these Downs. There are no known villas within the Marlborough Downs although there may have been villas around Upper Upham, and one existed at Littlecote to the east. Plentiful Roman remains have also been found around the village of Badbury one mile north-west of Liddington Hill, including a sarsen and chalk building with a tiled roof at Meadow Way which may have been a small villa. Dating was uncertain, but it was probably first or second century. Another Romano-British building was excavated near the Plough Inn at Chiseldon.

Roman settlement tended to gravitate to the watered valleys, but the downlands retained their importance as arable and pasture lands and were not deserted. They were probably inhabited by the humble native agricultural workers during the Romano-British period, just as in later times agricultural labourers were sometimes housed in cottages built beside the field barns in remote downland locations.

Romano-British settlements are known east of the Ridgeway at the south end of Overton Down, at Round Hill Downs, and at Upper Upham, the last two being towards Aldbourne. At Upper Upham Roman pottery was found at the centre of the tiny earthwork a little south of Upham Manor (at 228 768). Jefferies wrote of this earthwork 'somewhat south of the present mansion...on the very edge of the hill', and described it as 'a hollow in the ground, of a circular shape, which has four well marked entrances, and three tiers or steps, like a miniature amphitheatre', and concluded 'It is in short a cockpit'. The earthwork was evidently better preserved when Jefferies saw it in the 1860s than it now is. We should note that it was the Romans who introduced cockfighting into England, that this sport remained popular throughout the Medieval period, and that during the reign of the Stuarts it was known as 'the royal diversion'. James I, who owned Upper Upham, was said to attend at least two cock-fights a week. Richard Jefferies knew Upper Upham particularly well from writing the history of the Goddards who formerly held it, and he obtained much of his information from an elderly lady whose memory extended back into the eighteenth century. The well preserved state of this earthwork when Jefferies saw it may indicate that here we have a Roman cockpit which continued to be used as such until comparatively recent times.

A Roman building of some description existed near Manton House (170 704) and another west of Avebury (084 700). Roman coins and pottery were found in 1892 one mile west of Ogbourne Maizey (173 714) beside the minor road from that village to Old Eagle, and another Roman building existed on Barton Down three quarters of a mile from where the coins and pottery were discovered. Six Roman coins were also found by Professor Piggott in the forecourt of West Kennett Barrow where they were perhaps dropped by Roman visitors looking at the antiquities! On Martinsell a Romano-British rubbish heap was excavated early this century in Withy Copse outside the north-west corner of the hillfort, and three Roman cyst burials were discovered about thirty yards east of the Ridgeway on Overton Hill near the intersection of the Roman road and the Ridgeway (*WAM* 59). Another Romano-British burial dating from about 300 AD was found at the north-east end of Hackpen Hill (141 760) also associated with the Ridgeway, when an oil pipeline was laid in 1985.

From the evidence of these remains it is evident that the Romans – or more precisely the Romanised Britons – were present in this area which was exploited principally for grain. The limited extent of the Roman remains is a little surprising as a villa or two is to be expected in the Marlborough Downs, although their absence is consistent with the other great downland area of Wiltshire where, on Salisbury Plain, there is a complete lack of Roman villas except at the perimeter. In fact Richard Jefferies wrote in the *North Wilts Herald* in the 1860s of a mosaic pavement found on the hill above Lower Upham 'in a very perfect state of preservation', and reported its loss after the farmer had literally carted it around displaying it. This site may have been at the crossing of ways directly above Lower Upham (at 213 773) where there are earthworks along the hillside or, perhaps more probably, a little farther north along the track to Liddington Hill where A.D. Passmore found Roman artifacts in the 1920s (at 215 782).

The dearth of Roman antiquities must be explained by their taking over the existing system of agriculture and leaving it fundamentally unchanged, as did the Normans when they conquered Saxon England a thousand years after the Roman Conquest. This theory implies some continuity between the agriculture of the Iron Age and that of Medieval England, through the Romano-British, Anglo-Saxon and Norman periods.

Long Tom on Fyfield Down, the two-and-a-half metre tall monolith which stands on a parish boundary and used to be a prominent landmark on the open down when it was freestanding before it was obscured by an intrusive elder bush. Four Mile Clump is on the horizon. The elder bush has now (2003) been removed

4 The Historical Background

ANGLO SAXON (from mid 5th century to 1066 AD)

With the departure of the Roman army in about 410 AD and the abandonment of the province of Britain we leave the prehistoric period and enter the historic period when events in Britain began to be recorded in documents. This period has in the past been known as the Dark Ages and regarded as a period of decline following the breakdown of Roman civilisation, but modern scholarship generally inclines away from that assessment and the exquisite quality of much Anglo-Saxon and Viking art is now recognised. For a time after the departure of Roman troops the Romano-British civilians clung to their Romanised habits and civilisation, but progressively the incursions of the Anglo-Saxons increased as they first raided and then began to settle in Britain. When the Romans left they abandoned Britain. Five hundred years later, when King Alfred died, the country had become England. It should be emphasised that the Anglo-Saxon period in Wessex contained two distinct periods, the pagan Saxon and the subsequent Christian Saxon period which came about as a result of the Christianisation of Wessex which began with the mission of Bishop Birinus in about 635 AD.

Saxon Battles

During the pagan Saxon incursions into Britain at least two and possibly three major battles were fought in the Marlborough Downs. The first Saxons to settle in Britain were the mercenaries employed by Vortigern in Kent in the mid-fifth century. During the late-fifth and early-sixth centuries Saxon settlers began to expand west along the Thames Valley past Reading and Oxford. They were checked at the Battle of Mount Badon ('Mons Badonicus') between 480 and 500 – the date is uncertain since the defeat is not mentioned in the *Anglo-Saxon Chronicle* – which was fought somewhere south of the Upper Thames. The British leader at Mount Badon was said to have been Arthur who was probably a military commander under the Romano-British king Ambrosius Aurelius. The defeat of the Saxons was so decisive that for a period of about fifty years the advance was checked, a period of peace ensued, and there is evidence that at this time some Saxons returned to the Continent. The Battle of Mount Badon seems to have been associated with a hill fort. This may have been Badbury Hill camp west of Faringdon, but could equally well be Liddington Castle which was formerly known both as Battlesbury and Badbury Castle. The village of Baydon does not appear to be a probability because there is no hillfort directly associated with it.

Under pressure from the Anglo-Saxon invasions the Britons probably retired to the prehistoric hillforts such as Liddington, Bar-bury and Martinsell and defended them. The sixth century British historian Gildas wrote that in the fifth century many Romano-Britons did not flee but 'held out ... in their own land, trusting their lives with constant foreboding to the high hills, steep, menacing and fortified.'

From about 477 other Saxon invaders were appearing and in 495 a Saxon adventurer called Cerdic landed with his son Cynric at a place on the south coast recorded as *Cerdicesora*, conquered the immediate area, and founded a dynasty. These Saxons pushed north into Wiltshire, but their advance seems to have been gradual because it was not until 556 that the *Anglo-Saxon Chronicle* recorded: 'In this year (556) Cynric and Ceawlin fought against the Britons at *Beranburh*'. The *Chronicle* does not record that the Saxons won. The Battle of Beranburh, which ultimately led to a merger of the Upper Thames Saxons with the West Saxons, is generally accepted to have taken place at Barbury Castle. According to Henry of Huntingdon the British at *Beranburh* adopted Roman battle formations and very nearly won the day, but the Saxons finally triumphed. Ceawlin was the son of Cynric and grandson of Cerdic, and a few years after *Beranburh* he succeeded his father Cynric as king of Wessex in about 500 AD.

For a time there was still rivalry between the Upper Thames Saxons and the West Saxons, and in 592 Ceol – sometimes Ceolwulf – who had probably set up a kingdom south of Wansdyke, fought another Ceawlin at the Battle of *Wodnesbeorg* (Woden's Barrow), now known as Adam's Grave on Walker's Hill. It is relevant to note that Ceawlin claimed descent through Cerdic from both Adam and the Teutonic high god Woden, and both of their names are associated with the long barrow on Walker's Hill. This barrow stands near the strategic point called Red Shore where the Ridgeway meets Wansdyke. The *Anglo-Saxon Chronicle* for 592 reads: 'In this year there was a great slaughter at Adam's Grave, and Ceawlin was expelled'. He died the following year, and Ceol(wulf) ruled Wessex from 592-596 AD.

In 715 there was a Second Battle of Adam's Grave. The Anglo-Saxon Chronicle recorded: 'In this year Ine and Ceolred fought at Adam's Grave'. A hundred years later in 823 Egbert, king of Wessex, defeated Beornwulf, king of Mercia, at 'Ellandun' which is believed to be Wroughton, and by his victory established for a time the superiority of Wessex over Mercia.

When the Neolithic enclosure on Knap Hill was excavated early this century an Anglo-Saxon sword which may well have been a relic from this battle was found. Traces of Anglo-Saxon settlement were found at Avebury village and at East Kennett. Although there was no mention of a village at Avebury in Domesday, a small settlement existed there in the sixth century. A house with a sunken floor has been excavated immediately west of the embankment, and tenth and eleventh century buildings have also been found outside the west entrance to Avebury, indicating that Saxon occupation continued up to the Norman Conquest. A pre-Conquest church was built west of the stone circle probably after 900, and until 1811 both north and south walls of Avebury Church survived as Anglo-Saxon work. Two Saxon windows survive in the present church.

In 1962 five Anglo-Saxon bodies were found as secondary burials inserted into Bronze Age barrows on Overton Hill (*WAM* 80). They were two warriors, one woman, and two children. Saxon burials inserted into prehistoric barrows were a pagan Saxon practice and these burials were found to be fifth or sixth century. Another unexcavated Anglo-Saxon cemetery was in 1941 found at Fox Hill at the extreme north-west edge of the Marlborough Downs.

Wansdyke

The immense linear bank and ditch of Wansdyke runs west to east across the hills at the southern edge of the Marlborough Downs above Pewsey

Vale. The fact that the ditch is on its north side proves that Wansdyke was dug to defend the area south of the dyke from attack from the north, and excavation by General Pitt-Rivers proved it to be late-Roman or post-Roman since at one point it lies over a Roman road. Sections made by Colt Hoare revealed two periods of construction with an interval long enough for a substantial turf layer to develop over the initial rampart.

Anglo-Saxon land charters suggest that Wansdyke probably existed in 778, when there is reference to *quaddam vallum* meaning a certain dyke, and that it was certainly in existence in 825 when it was called *Ealden Dic* (Old Dyke). This implies that Wansdyke was old in 825, and there has been much speculation about its precise date. No secure date has yet been proved, but it seems likely that it was constructed by the Britons to block Saxon advance from the north in the late fifth century and was overtaken by events when other Saxons under Cynric and Ceawlin advanced from the south in the sixth century. The strategic point where the Ridgeway crosses Wansdyke (118 649) is known as Red Shore, shore meaning gap, from the red earth in this area.

Looking north through a gap – locally known as a 'shore' – in Wansdyke on Milk Hill. Silbury Hill is seen in the left middle distance.

An interesting point regarding Wansdyke is the fact that parish boundaries tend to cross it. Such boundaries usually made use of prominent existing features such as Roman roads and prehistoric linear earthworks to define their precise position. The fact that they ignore such a prominent line as Wansdyke virtually proves that the dyke post-dates the parish boundaries.

A number of writers have enthused about the pleasures of walking Wansdyke. O.G.S. Crawford suggested in *Archaeology in the Field* (1953) that; 'there would be no better beginning for a field archeologist than to walk Wansdyke from Morgan's Hill to near Marlborough ... There is, moreover, no finer downland in the whole of England, though no doubt it is doomed, like the rest, to be turned into arable'.

In *The Archaeology of Wessex* (1958) L.V. Grinsell wrote: 'The walk along the twelve miles or so of Wansdyke between Morgan's Hill and Savernake Forest provides one of the most spectacular experiences in British field archaeology'. It should perhaps be emphasised that this walk is best taken on a clear day in order that the magnificent views in all directions can be appreciated.

Viking Raids

From the eighth century Anglo-Saxon England was subjected to an increasing number of Viking raids from Scandinavia. Large parts of the country fell to them and despite the fact that Wessex was the single major Saxon Kingdom which successfully resisted the Viking assaults there is some evidence of Viking settlement in the Marlborough Downs. The now abandoned village of Snap west of Aldbourne was of early origin. Its name appears in a document of 1268 so that it may well have existed before the Norman Conquest. The name for me has a decidedly Viking sound; there is a *Snapparp* on the west coast of Sweden, and it is also significant that nearly all the other Snap and Snape names in Britain are in Viking settlement areas such as Suffolk, Yorkshire, Lancashire, Orkney and Shetland. Despite the undoubted fact of settlement by the Vikings in the Bristol Channel, where Steep Holme and Flat Holme are Viking names, suggestion of Viking settlements in the Marlborough Downs is rather original, but there is other place-name evidence. Burderop was in 1249 *Burithorp* (Assize Rolls) and *thorp* is without doubt a Viking suffix which appears in 1310 as *Hullethorp* for Hilldrop near Ramsbury, and also at Eastrop and Westrop at Highworth not far away. There were in fact strong links between Wessex and Norway. Athelstan – who ruled Wessex 925-939 – brought up at his court Haakon the Good who became king of Norway. Perhaps Haakon's attendants had holdings in the Marlborough Downs.

This area of Wiltshire was of some importance in the late Christian Saxon period and in 909 Ramsbury was created the bishopric from which most of Wiltshire and Berkshire was administered throughout the Norman period until the see merged with Sarum in the twelfth century. There is a tradition that Bishop Herman of Ramsbury assisted at the coronation of William the Conqueror to imply Saxon acceptance of William but there is no evidence for him having assisted at Westminster, although he may have done at a second coronation at the old Saxon capital of Winchester.

When the Danes invaded England in 1006 the *Anglo-Saxon Chronicle* records 'Then levies were mustered there at East Kennett, and there they joined battle; but the Danes soon put that force to flight, and bore their plunder to the sea'. In 'Ancient Wiltshire Battlefields' (*WAM* 53) Colonel A.H. Burne placed this battle 'astride the Ridgeway a few hundred yards north of the Kennet' on Overton Hill. If, as seems inevitable, the Danes were following the Ridgeway southwards after their raid on Wallingford in Berkshire, it would be logical for the Anglo-Saxon levies, having gathered at East Kennett, to bar their progress on Overton Hill north of the ford over the Kennet (120 677) and probably towards the top of the hill near the A4 in order that the Danes should not have the advantage of advancing downhill. Having forced the crossing of the Kennet, the Danish host went on past Winchester to their ships on the south coast, while Saxon burial parties buried the slain. In 1678 a number of bodies were found buried merely a foot underground about eighty yards east of The Sanctuary on Overton Hill.

Four years later, in 1010, Danish marauders were again back in this area, crossing the Marlborough Downs from the Thames to the Vale of Pewsey, presumably again using the Ridgeway. The *Anglo-Saxon Chronicle* records; '1010....Then before St. Andrew's day [30 November] the host came to Northampton and immediately destroyed the town by fire...and went thence across the Thames into Wessex and so on towards the marsh land at All and Bishop's Cannings, destroying everything with fire'. It was at this time that Silbury Hill was fortified as a strong point with palisades, and the Saxon burial which Stukeley found on its summit may date from this time.

The Anglo-Saxon settlement extended over about 600 years from 450 to 1066, a very long time when compared to the period 1300 to 1900. Many villages were founded as small settlements during this period, but have undergone great change since their original foundation. Of the four upland villages described in Chapter 7, all are mentioned in early documents. Rockley appears as *Rochelie* in 1086, Shaw as *Schaga* in 1165, Snap as Snape in 1268, and Upper Upham as *Uphameere* in 955. These references prove that two of the four existed in Saxon times, and that the other two are likely to have done.

Anglo-Saxon Estate Boundaries

Features of the Marlborough Downs which are of undoubted Anglo-Saxon origin are the boundaries of the Anglo-Saxon estates as recorded in the Anglo-Saxon charters. A one-inch to the mile map of Wiltshire showing the area covered by these charters is kept in the library of the Wiltshire Archaeological Society at Devizes, and a list of the existing charters giving both their location and the attempts to solve them is included in *WAM* 58. Several are relevant to the Marlborough Downs, and many have been worked over by Dr. G.B. Grundy of Oxford. Most of his solutions are regarded as valid but they should be used with caution since he worked from his study and neglected fieldwork.

The Saxon estate boundaries often became parish boundaries and Professor Hoskins has drawn attention to their survival at Alton Priors in the Vale of Pewsey on the south side of the Marlborough Downs where some of the boundary marks may still be seen. In Winding Combe (the Saxon *Woncomb*) there is reference in the charter to a stone with a hole in it, and until recently we could see this large sarsen almost nine feet across complete with hole which the Saxon surveyor took as his boundary marker in 825 when he defined the boundaries of this estate which King Egbert granted to a Winchester church. On Milk Hill above, behind the White Horse, stands the old dewpond known as Oxenmere which was mentioned in the same charter as *Oxnamere*. This pond takes its name from the fact that it stands on the Saxon boundary, *(ge)maere* meaning boundary, not from the fact that it is pond or mere. When I last saw Oxenmere in 2002 it was still holding water.

The Anglo-Saxon charter for Fyfield and West Overton parishes suggests that in the Saxon period the prehistoric farming on the upland area of the parishes on Fyfield and Overton Downs was continued on these marginal downlands in association with the valley-based economy of these parishes.

A final note on the Anglo-Saxon period in the Marlborough Downs concerns the unusual place-name of Man's Head (141 740) beside the minor road from Broad Hinton to Marlborough one mile west of Hackpen Hill. This is a small knoll, the 'head' element in its name arising just as the 'knap' element (*cnaepp* meaning knoll) arose in Knap Hill. Man's Head at the very heart of the Marlborough Downs may be the moot or meeting-place of the Selkley Hundred, the site of which has never been identified.

MEDIEVAL (from 1066 AD to about 1500 AD)

During the Medieval period there was less activity in the Downs, settlements having now generally moved into the valleys leaving the downlands as sheepwalks. There are nevertheless many areas of interest, one of which is the early Medieval castle mound of Lewisham Castle (243 738) two miles south-west of Aldbourne and commanding the crossing of the old road from Aldbourne to Marlborough and the way running south from Liddington Hill to Ramsbury, which was then a bishopric. We do not known precisely when Lewisham Castle was built but it is said to have obtained its name from Louis, Dauphin of France – alternatively Lewis – who was offered the throne of England when King John refused to implement the terms of Magna Carta. This derivation has been dismissed as fanciful, yet it is known that Louis campaigned around Marlborough in 1216 and may have put a garrison into Lewisham for the domination of the countryside by the occupation of its castles was an integral part of the strategy for that campaign.

Hugh de Neville surrendered Marlborough Castle to the the Dauphin in 1216 and that same year French troops devastated Savernake Forest. A passage in the novel *Richard Dumbledore* written in 1877 by the Rev. Richard Meyrick was based upon Aldbourne and reads:

> Tradition tells how, down along the straggling row of hovels which once stretched into the hills, at curfew time might be heard the clang of the iron gates at Lewisham Castle, which stood some two miles from the present village. But of the castle not one stone is left...

Medieval tiles have been found at Lewisham, but the lack of stone probably arises from the likelihood that at this early date the castle, (which is incidentally on private land with no public access), was of timber.

Religious Establishments

Early in the twelfth century a small alien Benedictine cell was founded at Avebury, but was dissolved in 1414. There were formerly Norman fragments at Avebury Manor which may have survived from this foundation. Another Benedictine Priory was formed at Ogbourne St. George in about 1149 and the Prior of Ogbourne features in many early documents. In 1241 he presented Henry III with three tuns of iron-flavoured wine, one being sent to Westminster, one to Windsor and the other to Winchester, which leads to speculation whether there was a vineyard at Ogbourne. Ogbourne Priory was founded by Maud of Wallingford as a cell to the Abbey of Bec in Normandy, and stood west of the present church.

At Clatford in the Kennet Valley was an alien priory which was a cell of the French abbey of St. Victor at Caux. This may have been deliberately sited at a prehistoric ritual site, for here was the Broadstones Ring of sarsens, mentioned by Aubrey and Stukeley, but destroyed in the 1880s. No sign survives today of the 'eight huge stones in a Circle' recorded by Aubrey.

The religious order of Knights Templar was founded in the early twelfth century to defend the pilgrim routes to Palestine. They were granted Rockley and Lockeridge in 1155 or 1156 and at Temple Farm (137 727) formed a preceptory of their order. Temple Farm is now confusingly Top Temple, Temple Farm having moved to the site formerly known as Temple Bottom Barn (148 724). The Templars only held Temple Farm for a little over a hundred and fifty years because their order was in 1309 suppressed in both France and England. On 18 February 1310 the Constable of

The hollowed out sarsen stone known as the Templar's Bath in Temple Bottom near Rockley. The sarsen is very large, measuring overall about 4.6 by 3 metres.

Marlborough Castle was directed, as a result of a bull issued by Pope Clement V directing an enquiry into the conduct of the Templars, to convey the local commander Walter de Rockley and his fellow Templars from Marlborough Castle to the Tower of London. At their suppression the Templar lands were given to the Knights Hospitallers of St. John, and it is interesting to note the apparent coincidence that in the early seventeenth century the St. John family provided MPs for Marlborough and that they became owners of Rockley.

The Gloucester poet Ivor Gurney (1890-1937) wrote:

> 'One finds the strangest things in walks, ...
> Old troughs, great stone cisterns bishops might have blessed'

and in Temple Bottom a little west of Rockley can be found such a trough or cistern which is one of the strangest things to be seen in the Marlborough Downs. About thirty yards south of the track along the bottom, on a little green between a modern house and a tennis court, there lies (at 143 725) a very large sarsen stone which has been artificially hollowed into a large depression with a drainage hole bored through two feet (60cm) of solid sarsen. This stone was noted by A.D.Passmore in 1924 (*WAM* 51) as being known locally as the Templar's Bath. Its purpose is not known; it may formerly have served some perfectly utilitarian purpose in these waterless downs, such as cheesemaking which we know took place on this Templar site. Alternatively it may have been housed in a timber building which has now perished, and been used in Templar rituals or as a baptismal trough. It should be remembered that bathing was of eastern origin and among many oriental peoples it was a religious rite which the Templars may have brought back from their campaigning in the east.

Glory Ann

The presence of the Knights Templar in these Downs may explain the mysterious place-name Glory Ann (128 727) which has been the subject of much speculation among etymologists literally for centuries. The name has been omitted from recent maps, although it survived on the Ordnance Survey until recent times. Glory Ann is now merely an isolated pond on Hackpen Hill which was dredged and reconstructed in 1991, but it was formerly a place of some activity. Nearby in prehistoric times was the Old Chapel barrow and mortuary enclosure described by Stukeley in the eighteenth century. In 1773 Andrews and Dury marked 'Glory Ann' on their map of Wiltshire, and in the early nineteenth century Colt Hoare (in *Ancient Wiltshire* Vol. 2) referred to 'a cottage adjoining the trackway referred to by the fanciful title of Glory Ann'. Interest in the strange place-name was beginning, and on his map of 1820 Greenwood marked 'Glory Ann or Port Lorien'. The 'port' element in a country district normally indicates a way to a market town, and it seems probable that 'Glory Ann' may be the Wiltshire peasants' attempt to pronounce 'Port Lorien'. This suggestion is quite feasible when one considers that St. Anne's Hill above Pewsey Vale became corrupted into Tan Hill. But why Port Lorien?

Later in the nineteenth century the antiquarian Rev. A.C. Smith noted 'The strange name of Glory Ann, which has been a sore puzzle to antiquarians', and also recorded that the earthworks at Glory Ann were injured when 'a cattle yard was formed here'. This supports 'port' meaning a way to a market, for Glory Ann stands near the point where a droveway branches south-east from the Ridgeway making for Marlborough and its fairs. It is evident that formerly the two ponds, cottage and barn at Glory Ann provided watering and a stopping place for drovers and their herds and flocks, as did the pond and cottage at Old Totterdown (138 718) a mile south-east of Glory Ann down the same track.

Speculation continued. In 1911 Edward Thomas mentioned the etymological problems raised by the name in his foreword to Isaac Taylor's *Words and Places* where he wrote: 'It may well be as long a chase as that after the Glory Ann who gave her name to a barn near the Icknield Way on Hackpen Hill in Wiltshire.' At that time the A4361 road from Avebury to Swindon was believed to be the Icknield Way, and was marked as such by O.G.S. Crawford (in his *Archaeology in the Field*) as late as 1953.

The presence of the Templars half a mile east of Glory Ann suggests a Templar connection. The 'orient' was the east, where the Templars were active on their Crusades, but a possible explanation may be found in the last word of the Templar motto which read 'Non nobis, Domine, non nobis, sed Nomini Tuo da gloriam' ('Bestow glory not to us, O Lord, not to us but to Thy Name')

Wroughton Copse Settlement

About a mile south of the Templar preceptory in Temple Bottom an early Medieval settlement existed on Fyfield Down immediately south of Wroughton Copse (at 137 707). Wroughton is another corruption, this time from *Raddun* meaning Red Down from the red-brown clay-with-flints which overlays the chalk in this area. In 1248 it was *Raddon* in a Winchester document, the site being then in the ownership of the Prior of St. Swithin's at Winchester. Finds proved occupation from 1100 to 1300 and records prove that the farming at Raddon was principally sheep husbandry. Excavation by Professor Fowler in the early 1960s discovered a long house, that being a long single-story building occupied by humans at one end and animals at the other. The interim reports are in *WAM* 58 and 59 and include photographs. *Raddon* was 'Rowden' on Andrews and Dury (1773) and 'Rodden' in the 1814 Enclosure Award. The site was surrounded by an embankment which may still be seen on the ground. Nearby there was another Medieval settlement at The Beeches (148 717) on Clatford Down.

Rabbit Warrens

Two important features of the Medieval landscape were the rabbit warrens and the deer parks which provided fresh meat during the winter months when only breeding livestock could be kept because of the scarcity of winter fodder. Rabbit warrens existed in the Marlborough Downs at a number of locations which included Aldbourne Warren, Liddington Warren, the warrens along the south edge of the Downs above Pewsey Vale, and there was also a large hare warren on Marlbrough Common from which hares were in 1232 sent to Reading for the king's table. This warren subsequently became a rabbit warren. Such rabbit warrens are known to have existed at least from the fourteenth century and, since rabbits were introduced into England by the Normans, they almost certainly existed earlier. Rabbits were sent from Aldbourne Warren for the table of Henry IV who reigned 1399-1413 and would have been familiar with this warren which was owned by his father John of Gaunt as part of the Duchy of Lancaster estates. Aubrey was very complimentary about the quality of the rabbits from Aldbourne Warren in the seventeenth century, and the warrens generally continued in existence up to the Napoleonic Wars when they tended to be ploughed up for arable crops. An advertisement in the *Salisbury and Winchester Journal* in 1812 sought for a tenant to convert 780 acres of Aldbourne Warren into arable at a time when rents for arable land were fifty per cent more than for warren land. It must have been soon after 1812 that Aldbourne Warren was ploughed. On 4 January 1878 Richard Jefferies wrote in *The Livestock Journal* that 'Aldbourne warren is still remembered, and the rabbits are said to have consumed several loads of hay a day in frosty and snowy weather'. Immediately south of the track which runs west out of the B4192 half a mile north-west of Aldbourne to the Giant's Grave barrow (at 246 764), the old wall of Aldbourne Warren may still be seen.

Associated with the subject of rabbit warrens are pillow mounds. These are large low mounds usually pillow-shaped and only up to three feet high. They are frequently surrounded by ditches which provided material for the mound. Sometimes they have been mistaken for prehistoric works and even marked as long barrows on the maps. Their purpose has been a matter of some speculation, but O.G.S. Crawford concluded that they were created in Medieval times for rabbits to burrow into, and that theory

Wall of large sarsen stones at The Beeches west of Rockley, probably surviving from the Medieval settlement at this site.

has now been generally accepted. There is a case at Danebury in Hampshire where the rabbit runs were actually dug for them and then shuttered over and back-filled with earth, creating the novel situation of round rabbits in square holes! Several examples of pillow mounds may be seen in the Marlborough Downs including some on Sugar Hill (235 788) and one beside the Workway Drove (116 637) under Knap Hill. Both are associated with areas known to have been rabbit warrens. The last is marked 'tumuli' on some maps. Excavation suggests that no pillow mounds date from earlier than the sixteenth century.

Deer Parks

Medieval deer parks are not much in evidence in the Marlborough Downs since they demanded wooded areas, deer being essentially woodland animals. All linear earthworks are not prehistoric, although many such Medieval banks and ditches have been assumed to be prehistoric. Early deer parks were almost invariably surrounded by banks and ditches with a park-pale fence on the bank. The only possible Medieval deer park in these Downs is that which may have been made north-west of Upper Upham Manor when it was a hunting lodge for Aldbourne Chase. The linear earthwork which is seen looking north from point 223 773 on the track between Lower and Upper Upham could in my opinion be the remains of a park-pale which extends for some distance north-west of Upper Upham. The creation of a deer park in this position may explain the early abandonment of the old village of Upper Upham (225 774).

Other definite deer parks existed at the edges of these Downs. There were two at Ramsbury Manor and another at Burderop Park at the north edge of the Marlborough Downs. Here the bank and ditch which follows the east side of the B4005 (from 163 804 to 163 801) is probably a park-pale, and if so it is the best preserved in Wiltshire.

Strip Lynchets

Strip Lynchets are often Medieval. They are cultivation terraces formed on a hillside as a result of cultivation causing earth to be displaced downhill. As a result terraces are formed between positive and negative lynchets. Strip lynchets, which are normally long and narrow, may have originated earlier than the Medieval period in Anglo-Saxon or even prehistoric times but they are generally regarded as Medieval because they were extensively used at that time. Examples of such lynchets are found on Easton Hill (063 648) north of Horton, and on the south side of Giant's Grave (164 630) above the village of Oare. The unusual place-name Michael's Lynch (153 727) which is shown on the maps applied to a steep slope half a mile north-west of Rockley presumably refers to a lynchet which was either owned or worked by a person called Michael.

Enclosures

Earthwork enclosures dating from the Medieval period are present in the Marlborough Downs. One of the best, which is also easily seen, is the example on Burderop Down (160 764) overlaying a prehistoric field system. It is seen on the left as you approach Barbury Castle by the road south from Wroughton and Burderop.

A number of rectangular enclosures are associated with Wansdyke, on for example Morgan's Hill (040 670), Horton Down (078 661), and All Cannings Down (091 652). Excavation by Mrs. Cunnington of the example on Morgan's Hill concludes that these enclosures are Medieval. Of it she wrote: 'the enclosure was used as a fold or penning for flocks, chiefly perhaps for sheep, the inner enclosure affording additional protection for the weak and sickly ones, and perhaps for the shepherds'. These enclosures and their relationship to Wansdyke have been the subject of some speculation, but it seems likely that they were holding enclosures for droves approaching Tan Hill Fair site along Wansdyke which was a convenient well-defined route for getting to the fair in its remote situation.

Roads and Trackways

In the Medieval period roads and trackways were generally unsurfaced and often not defined. Early in this period most travellers walked or rode horseback across unenclosed countryside, and goods were generally moved by packhorses. With the advent of more wheeled traffic in the shape of carts, wagons and coaches, ways became very bad. Attempts where made to limit wear on them by restricting the number of horses which could be used to draw each vehicle, and carts were required to have wide wheel treads. Rivers were generally crossed by fords rather than bridges.

Cattle moving diagonally uphill often cut 'hollow-ways' in the hillside.

Examples of such hollow-ways are frequent, and may be seen in this area at the rise from the west up Hackpen Hill (127 751). Here the modern road designed for wheeled traffic softens the gradient by taking a wide loop, but Medieval ways diverge from the road as distinct hollow-ways which slant into the Ridgeway from both sides of the present road.

POST-MEDIEVAL (from 1500 AD to about 1850)

Under this heading of Post-Medieval I propose to deal with some aspects of the history and the appearance of the Marlborough Downs from Medieval until comparatively modern times up to about 1850. During this period the move away from the Downs continued and they became less frequented.

Downland Farming

As men gravitated to the valley settlements and to the towns, and traffic routes took to the valleys. The high downland continued to be used as sheepwalks for the vast numbers of sheep which proliferated during the Medieval and post-Medieval periods under the system known as the 'sheep and corn husbandry' under which sheep fed on the Downs during the day and at night were folded on the cornlands to fertilise them with their manure.

Field barns were at this time built in remote situations in the Downs, often with one or two cottages associated with them, in order that the labourers and stockmen could live on the spot to attend to their animals. Such barns and cottages were built in many places in the Downs, for example at Glory Ann and Martinsell Hill, and sometimes appear on the map as 'Hill Barn', 'Field Barn', or 'Down Barn'. A good surviving example of such a barn, but lacking a cottage, may be seen at Wick Bottom Barn (147 732) north-west of Rockley.

On Overton Down a farmstead was built in the seventeenth century (at 134 707) a little south of Delling Copse, as a successor to the Medieval Wroughton Copse Settlement. This must have been one of the few farmsteads to be built high in the Marlborough Downs in this period.

Trees, usually beech, were planted in the hills, often in clumps for decorative purposes. Such clumps planted for no apparent reason became known as 'follies', as for example in Liddington Folly. In *Greene Ferne Farm* Richard Jefferies wrote: 'Every hill seems to have a folly. I mean a clump of trees on the top'. Trees were also planted in lines as shelter belts, and in copses as game-coverts (Delling Copse on Overton Down). Scots pine were planted as markers for droveways, for example along the track which runs east from Barbury along Burderop Down (164 764).

Rabbits continued to be extensively farmed in warrens such as Liddington and Aldbourne Warrens, until the warrens were ploughed for arable in the early nineteenth century to feed the populace during the Napoleonic Wars.

In the early seventeenth century a late example of a post-Medieval deer park was created between West Woods and Savernake over the still open area south of Marlborough. Before 1597 a park called Clatford Park (164 661) is mentioned as 'recently enclosed'. It had belonged to Sir Thomas Wroughton who died in 1597, but had been sold to Richard Goddard of the rising family of Goddards. In the 1583 *Notes of Parks in the County of Wilts* there is reference to a deer park at Clatford belonging to 'Mr. Goddarde' as being three miles in circuit, that is a circle one mile in diameter. The name of Clatford Park survives in Clatford Park Farm (164 661) with Park Farm half a mile to its south. The park was finally disparked in 1631, Savernake Great Park having been created immediately east of it in the early 1600s. Savernake had passed into the ownership of the Earl of Hertford whose father Protector Somerset had been executed under Edward VI. James I was a great hunter and had followed the example of his predecessors by hunting Savernake. It was probably at the instigation of James I, who was not above leaning on his courtiers to provide him with hunting facilities, that Hertford created Savernake Great Park. It covered an area about 2000 acres – which is an area about two miles in diameter – and its bounds ran approximately along the line of the A345 to its north-west, the A346 to the north-east, and along the road from Hat Gate through Wootton Rivers to Clench Common to the south. The area is marked 'Savernake or Savernake Great Park' on the 1773 map by Andrews and Dury. This area formerly covered by Savernake Great Park between Martinsell Hill and Marlborough remains a strange unfrequented area, despite the fact that it is criss-crossed by many public footpaths.

Civil War

Warfare reappeared in the Marlborough Downs during the Civil War after a long period of peace. Soon after the Battle of Roundway Down, which was fought a little west of the Marlborough Downs in July 1643 and was followed by the Royalist successes of the 'royalist summer', the Parliamentary Lord General Essex led a large army of trained bands out of London and succeeded in raising the siege of Gloucester which was being conducted by the Royal army. Having raised the seige, Essex was faced with getting his army consisting of about 10,000 foot, 4,000 cavalry and between 15 and 20 field guns back to London. After feinting towards Worcester, Essex moved south through Cirencester. It is difficult to believe that the king was so inept as to lose a hostile army of this size, but that is precisely what happened. Essex continued his march east. On 16 September 1643 he was at Cricklade, and on the 17th at Chiseldon. Prince Rupert's cavalry patrols were scouring the country, and on 18 September the Royalist Colonel Sir John Hurry – currently a Royalist although he changed sides several times during the Civil War and was finally executed for it – found Essex and his column marching along the little valley which runs from Snap east to Aldbourne through Aldbourne Chase. To give an idea of the length of column, if we ignore the 4,000 cavalry which would probably be to the sides forming screens, 10,000 foot marching in column-of-route three abreast at intervals of six feet would extend over three and three-quarters miles, which is more than the distance from Upper Upham to Aldbourne.

The Royalist cavalry numbering some 6,000 horse massed on the ridge near Dudmore Lodge (236 755) (which is 'Duddon Lodge' in a contemporary account) and harried the progress of the Parliamentary army along the valley. The action was 'very sharp for an hour or two' (Clarendon), and at about the site of Lodge Lower Barn which did not then exist, Essex formed his infantry into circles – not then squares – to repel the cavalry charges. He fired his 'drakes' (3-pound field pieces) into Prince Rupert's massed cavalry on the down near Dudmore Lodge. For long the Ordnance Survey placed the crossed swords indicating the battle site on the hill (at about 230 756) because this was where shot were found. King Charles was unable to bring up his infantry which had been left far behind as a result of the feint by Essex, and the Parliamentary army got safely back to

London after an indecisive action at Newbury. Those troops constituted the last surviving Parliamentary field army in the south of England, and had they failed to return to London there is little doubt that the king would have won the Civil War, but in this secluded little valley in Aldbourne Chase he missed his opportunity and lost the war, with immense consequences for the future history of England.

The route by which Essex led his army over the north-east edge of the Marlborough Downs from Chiseldon to Aldbourne was probably over the west shoulder of Liddington Hill and past Liddington Folly (203 791) to the crossing of ways (213 773) between Lower and Upper Upham, east through Upper Upham, down Heydown Drove to the valley (at 228 764), and then east along the valley past Lodge Lower Barn site to Aldbourne.

Two years later another event occurred in the Marlborough Downs which had a decisive influence upon the outcome of the Civil War. Shortly before the Battle of Naseby which took place in June 1645 and at which the New Model Army effectively won the war by decisively defeating the royal army, the royal commander in the west, Lord Goring, was ordered by Prince Rupert to bring his cavalry to a rendezvous with the king's army at Market Harborough in the Midlands. Goring nominated Tan Hill as the muster point. Waylen records in his *History Military and Municipal of the Town of Marlborough* (1854):

> Previous to Naseby fight, Lord Goring having been summoned out of the West, to join the royal standard, and to gather on his way such troops as he had left in Wilts, came through Devizes on the lst of May, and appointed the conspicuous eminence of Tan Hill as a rendezvous. His numbers swelled to 3,000, with whom he marched during the following night to a spot called 'Marlborough Thorns'.

Having commenced his march north-east – probably along Wansdyke and through Marlborough and Hungerford – Goring decided to disobey orders and stay in the west. He was going through a bad patch, two divisions of his army having recently fought a brisk action for two hours, each under the misapprehension that the other was a Parliamentary army, an event which the unrepentant Goring dismissed as 'the most fantastical accident since the war began'. Goring lingered around Newbury, and sent off a dispatch to Prince Rupert indicating that he would not be coming north. This dispatch was intercepted, and its contents led Fairfax to bring on the action at Naseby which won the war. After Naseby, Goring drew the Western Army back towards Taunton, and it was dispersed by Fairfax with a very much superior force at the Battle of Langport on 11 July 1645.

Sporting Activity

During the seventeenth, eighteenth and nineteenth centuries the Marlborough Downs were the venue for a number of sporting activities. Remote places in the Downs were resorted to for wrestling matches and prize fights, as described by Alfred Williams. Wrestling was of such ferocity that its participants were forbidden to attach iron tips to their boots in order to avoid severe injuries when they kicked their opponents, and prize fights were often fought by professional pugilists and were equally fierce, being continued until one of the contestants was so injured that he could not continue. Williams also recorded the recollections of old men to their backswording with singlesticks. This was a kind of degenerate rustic fencing. He also tells of the injuries they sustained when indulging this popular sport, and of the resorting to the public house afterwards for bread, cheese and ale, which regaled the spectators and revived the participants.

Another favourite sport was cockfighting which has already been mentioned in connection with Upper Upham. This was also a very popular sport in the downland areas. All of these sporting activities were very much associated with gambling, as was horse-racing. The early horse-race meetings of the eighteenth century were essentially regional and were popular with all classes of people. They drew competitors and spectators from miles around, a race-meeting being a great social event as is revealed by reports in early newspapers. Three racecourses are known to have existed in the Marlborough Downs, all being closely associated with the Swindon to Marlborough Turnpike road past Four Mile Clump which provided easy access to them.

On their 1773 map of Wiltshire, Andrews and Dury show 'Marlborough Race' (centre about 169 742) a little south of the point later occupied by

Four Mile Clump, which then did not exist. This course may already in 1773 have been about to move to a new location nearer Marlborough since the same map shows 'Marlborough New Race' on Barton Down between Rockley and Marlborough (centre 168 708). Subsequently Manton House was built as a racehorse training establishment at an old crossing of downland ways, and adopted 'Marlborough New Race' as its training gallops.

Burderop Racecourse, also known as Mudgell racecourse, was later opened a little north of Barbury Castle and astride the Ridgeway (at 166 774). This racecourse is shown on both Greenwood's 1820 map and the first Ordnance Survey of about the same date as 'Burdrop Race Course'. Mudgell has become Midge Hall on recent maps. *The Place-Names of Wiltshire* ignores Mudgell, as do Andrews and Dury and the first Ordnance Survey, but to me it seems a pity to lose the old name for the more pretentious modern one. Records reveal that meetings were held from at least 1811 to 1831 at Burderop Racecourse under the auspices of Thomas Calley of Burderop Park. There was a small timber stand only fifteen feet long which ultimately went to Burderop Farm as a farm building when it was no longer needed at the racecourse. Although meetings seem to have ended at Burderop before he was born in 1848, Richard Jefferies gave a good account of this racecourse in his novel *World's End* written in 1877:

> Yet World's End was not altogether to be despised. In this out-of-the-way place there was perhaps the finest natural race-course in England, to which the uneven uphill course at Epsom, made famous by the Derby, was but an exercise ground.
>
> A level stretch of sweet, elastic turf, half a mile wide, ran in a line something like half a horseshoe, under the steep Downs, for a distance of two miles, unimpeded by hedge, ditch, or enclosed field, and obstructed only in a few spots by thick bushes of furze and a few scattered hawthorn trees. A spectator standing upon the Downs has the whole of this Plain, as it was called, at once under his eye; could see a horse start and watch it gallop to the goal. From an ancient earthwork camp or 'castle', this Down was known as Berbury Hill, and the level plain was often called Berbury racecourse.

Jefferies continued to explain that advertising a race-meeting was of little importance since 'The day was well known to all those who were likely to attend'.

For the upper classes in the seventeenth and probably early eighteenth centuries deer hunting on horseback was a favourite recreation. This involved chasing wild deer 'at large' over the open Downs. John Aubrey was taking part in such a deer hunt with some Royalist friends when he discovered the stone circle at Avebury. Fox hunting gradually supplanted deer hunting, and Sir Hugh Smyth, Bart. (1772-1824) lived much of his life at Rockley because of the excellent fox hunting, and kennelled his hounds in the village. Coursing for hares also took place on these Downs, especially between about 1799 and 1804 around Rockley (*Victoria County History 4*).

Tan Hill Fair was held annually throughout this period as a very popular pleasure fair associated with the stock fair to which droves of sheep, cattle and horses were driven for long distances over the downs along the remote droveways, some say guided by bonfires lighted before dawn at the site (083 648) above Pewsey Vale. As its 1499 charter recorded, the fair was held on 'the feast and morrow of St. Anne, August 6th-7th', and the local people flocked to the fair where cider, beer and cheese were on sale. The files of the *Wiltshire Gazette* contain many references to Tan Hill Fair, including a comment in 1860 that 'The gypsy tribe always abound at the Fair and offer amusements such as throwing at snuffboxes etc'.

White Horses

The fashion for chalk-cut figures in which the topsoil of the hillside was stripped away to expose the underlying chalk has manifested itself in the Marlborough Downs by a number of White Horses, although all of the examples in this area are comparatively modern. Such White Horses are a peculiarly Wiltshire phenomenon, although the first – which may be a dragon – was cut at Uffington in Berkshire probably in the Iron Age. They may have been first suggested by badger scrapes in the hillside which must have resembled some recognisable object. The best known in the Marlborough Downs is probably the Alton Barnes White Horse which was formed on the southern slope of Milk Hill in 1812 at the instigation of a Mr. Pile, a farmer who commissioned an itinerant artist called Jack the Painter to cut the figure and paid him £20 in advance. But Jack was a little too itinerant! He absconded with the £20 before completing the horse. Edward Thomas disliked 'the very tame looking White Horse above Alton Barnes' and suggested that it should be used to 'advertise horse food or embrocation', but I consider it to be one of the better examples and certainly the best in the Marlborough Downs.

Alton Barnes White Horse on Milk Hill and Walker's Hill (right) viewed from the Vale of Pewsey.

The Cherhill and Pewsey White Horses are outside the limits of our area so that, apart from the rather urban White Horse which a schoolmaster called Greasley cut into Granham Hill at the south-west end of Marlborough in 1804, the only other surviving examples in the Marlborough Downs are the horse which was cut in 1864 by Mr. William Saunders of Little Town on Broad Town Hill (098 782), and the White Horse which was formed in 1838 in the west face of Hackpen Hill where the Broad Town to Marlborough road climbs the hill by Mr. Henry Eatwell, a parish clerk. Both of these are inferior examples. Another White Horse existed beside the beech belt (at 153 733) on Rockley Down. This apparently nineteeth century example was visible from the Swindon to Marlborough turnpike near Four Mile Clump, but had been forgotten by all but the oldest shepherds when its outline was exposed by the plough in 1948.

This White Horse has now been lost again, having been frequently ploughed.

Country people are understandably fond of these landmarks with which they have been familiar since childhood, but sentimental attachment for an element of a landscape is not necessarily related to its aesthetic quality and I believe that in no case is this more evident than with the White Horses of Wiltshire. William Morris considered that Westbury White Horse 'somewhat spoils the headland', and the cutting of hill-figures can be carried to excess. Some years ago there was proposal to cut a figure of Marilyn Monroe as a fitting companion for the ancient Cerne Giant in Dorset.

Kennett Ale

In the eighteenth century ale from West Kennett gained a high reputation in many parts of England. Its fame spread as a result of travellers on the London to Bath road, which ran through the village, sampling it at the local inn. Robert Southey mentioned in *Letters from England*; 16 September 1802' that 'Kennett ale' was 'the best beer in England' and that it 'first came into repute in 1789, and many thousands of barrels of it are sent annually to London and to all parts of the country'. The brewing of Kennett ale seems to have taken place at West Kennett Farm where a malthouse was included in a lease dated 1745. This became a small brewery which survived until 1931.

Water Meadows

One of the most important developments in downland agriculture during the post-Medieval period was the invention of water meadows. These were lowland meadows adjoining rivers over which water was diverted by a series of carrier ditches, drains and sluices in a carefully regulated manner to provide an early flush of grass for sheep to eat. It may be thought that water meadows are not relevant to a book on downland, but they became an essential part of the downland 'sheep and corn husbandry' in which sheep were removed from the downs to obtain an 'early bite' of grass in the water meadows in March and April when hay was running out and normal grass was not yet in growth. Water meadows were very common in south Wiltshire but also appeared associated with the River Kennet. They were invented probably in the seventeenth century and Aubrey recorded: 'Watering of meadows about Marleburgh and so to Hungerford was, as I

Silbury Hill from the Winterbourne to its east, showing one of the carrier ditches to the former water meadows of this area

remember, about 1646'.

In a letter to his sister in 1849 William Morris describes walking through a water meadow between Avebury and Silbury Hill which must have been associated with the Winterbourne that feeds the Kennet. In case his sister did not appreciate what a water meadow was, the fifteen-year-old Morris wrote (and I hope that his education at Marlborough College included instruction in punctuation):

> I will tell you what a delectable affair a water meadow is to go through; in the first place you must fancy a field cut through with an infinity of small streams say about four feet wide each the people to whom the meadow belongs can turn these streams on and off when they like and at this time of year (April) they are on just before they put the fields up for mowing the grass being very long you cannot see the water till you are in the water and floundering in it except you are above the field luckily the water had not been long when we went through it else we would have been up to our middles in mud, however perhaps you can now imagine a water meadow.

The management of water meadows was an intricate business conducted by men known as 'drowners'. Such meadows continued to be managed and operated into the twentieth century, but water meadows generally declined with the introduction in the second half of the nineteenth century of the artificial fertilizers which provided alternative means of obtaining the vital early grass. Today the former water meadows on the Kennet near Silbury, and at Overton, Fyfield and Manton, are hardly recognisable although they occasionally become very evident in wet winters. During the period of heavy rainfall in late 1992 water stood in the shallow carriers and drains of the old water meadows and made them very visible.

Agrarian Riots

In 1830 the agrarian unrest which raged through most of southern England appeared in the Marlborough district. In general it was provoked by low wages in agriculture and the loss of rights under enclosure, but the immediate spark in 1830 was the threat to the poor living of the agricultural workers posed by the introduction of threshing machines which would take away their winter employment. The labourers of Wiltshire already were suffering from particularly low wages, and the 'Swing' riots – so-called because threatening letters were signed 'Captain Swing' – spread into Wiltshire on 15 November. In the period 15-28 November there was rioting, rick-burning, and smashing of threshing machines at many places, including the Marlborough district . To their eternal credit not a single person was seriously hurt by the rioters despite great provocation and the lack of an effective police force.

An incident which occurred at Rockley may be taken as typical of the events of the rising. Here a mob of some forty to fifty men assembled and were confronted by Mr. Thomas Mynors Baskerville, Justice of the Peace and Sheriff of Wiltshire, and a number of special constables including a Mr. Codrington. Among the rioters was Peter Withers, a man of twenty-three born at Chilton Foliat and the father of five children. There was a scuffle and Withers was alleged to have thrown a hammer at Mr. Codrington, although he pleaded self-defence after Mr. Codrington had attacked him with a whip. The incident took place on 23 November 1830, and the trial at Salisbury was on 7 January 1831. It was reported in *The Times* on 10 January. Withers was found guilty and sentenced to death but the sentence was commuted to transportation for life. Withers went to Tasmania where on 13 May 1836 he married Ann Wade. He was conditionally pardoned on 5 April 1838. These agrarian riots were put down with considerable severity in an attempt to ensure that they did not precipitate revolution on the scale which had been seen in France forty years before. The dependents of the transported farm labourers suffered great hardship from the loss of their breadwinners, but by the next year the countryside was quiet again and the remaining farm workers were back at work again with no appreciable improvement in their conditions.

Downland Hauntings

The agrarian riots of 1830 bring us up to modern times but, before leaving the history of the Marlborough Downs, mention should be made of several tales of downland hauntings which are associated with that history.

Two shepherds, Tod Beak and George Tasker, claimed to have seen one night a horse-drawn funeral cortege with a gold circlet on the coffin and lighted by many flambeaux proceeding along Wansdyke over Tan Hill.

The shepherds can have had little knowledge of the Arthurian legends, but it has since been suggested that they must have seen a manifestation of the funeral procession of Queen Guinevere as her corpse was conveyed by Sir Lancelot and eight companions on a horse bier from Amesbury, where she had died at the nunnery, to Glastonbury for interment beside her husband King Arthur. According to Mallory, writing much later in the early Middle Ages, 'an hundred torches were ever burning about the corpse of the queen'. In fact Wansdyke provides a particularly indirect way from Amesbury to Glastonbury, being fifteen miles north of the direct line which runs east from Amesbury past Warminster, but it is not impossible that in those unsettled times Guinevere's cortege may have taken an indirect way over the Downs to avoid the Saxon raiders against whom the late Arthur had campaigned.

A visitor to Adam's Grave on Walker's Hill in 1965 reported hearing the hoofbeats of massed galloping horses, although quite unaware that two major battles took place here in the Saxon period, in both of which cavalry would have taken part. The story of the haunting of Pit Pond at Huish, and Edith Olivier's ghostly experience at Avebury are mentioned elsewhere in this book.

As far as I am aware no ghost stories are told in connection with the former Templar presence in Temple Bottom east of Hackpen, and I am extremely sceptical about all such tales, but the deserted site at Glory Ann has long had an evil reputation and I must admit to sometimes feeling a sense of foreboding when alone at this remote place. I occasionally have been alone at Snap as dusk fell at the end of a day of walking in the Downs. As the sun sets and gloom gathers about the deserted village the presence can be imagined of the generations of villagers who for at least six hundred years eked out an impoverished existence in this remote downland coombe and have now gone without trace. Alone in the deserted village it is easy to imagine the presence of old Rachel Fisher, the last resident, pottering in her garden at the bend in the lane which was once the village street, where her snowdrops still bloom every spring. At such times my scepticism about the supernatural tends to be overcome by the melancholy which seems to linger in places long inhabited but now deserted, a melancholy which is aptly expressed by John Masefield in the poem quoted on page 140.

The dry bed of the River Kennet at East Kennett road bridge in October 1992. the following month, after a period of heavy rain, the water level reached the crown of the arches, which emphasises the intermittent rate of flow of the River Kennet

5 Climate, Flora and Fauna

Climate

Records at the Meteorological Office indicate that the climate of the Marlborough Downs is slightly warmer in summer and rather colder in winter than most parts of southern England. On these Downs the summer heat tends to be alleviated by the fresh breezes which also contribute to the lower temperatures in winter. Botanists have noted that the season in the Marlborough Downs tends to be a few weeks later than nearby areas such as the Salisbury district. The sunshine hours are considerably above average, and rainfall is moderate amounting to about thirty-three inches a year.

For long the pure air of the Wiltshire Downs has been regarded as health-giving. Much of our knowledge of the archaeology of Wiltshire is due to the fact that William Cunnington (1754-1810) was advised by his doctors because of ill health to 'breathe the salutary air of the Wiltshire Downs'. Having been advised to 'ride out or die' and having understandably elected to do the former, Cunnington devoted his time, in association with Colt Hoare of Stourhead, to researching, excavating and recording the prehistoric antiquities of Wiltshire, an activity in which he was succeeded by several later Cunningtons with distinction.

Anyone who would know the Marlborough Downs should try to see them at all seasons and in all weathers. Having generally become urbanised we have lost our rural roots, and with them the countryman's knowledge and appreciation of weather. 'All weathers are good to those who love the open air, and have their special attractions' wrote W.H. Hudson of another part of Wiltshire, and the character of these Downs will be found to vary immensely when seen in different weathers and at various seasons of the year.

The greatest deterrent to going out to the Downs is rain. For several years I was employed as a Ridgeway warden in the Marlborough Downs and was committed to going out on specific days all year round; in other words I was unable to choose my weather, and yet of all those days it is remarkable how few were washed out by rain. Great resolution is required to set out for a downland walk in the rain, although it is not so bad when it rains after you have started, yet whenever I have ventured out on marginal days – even when it has rained – I have almost invariably enjoyed my day. I recall one day in 1982 leading a walk and seeing from the exposed area at Glory Ann what appeared to be a solid wall of water bearing down from the direction of Avebury. Myfanwy Thomas – Edward Thomas's 'daughter the younger' – was in the group and I recall ruefully reminding her of a saying of her father's: 'At all times I love rain'. We all got very wet, but soon the sun came out and we dried out on steaming sarsen stones which took the sun's heat. For the rest of the day we enjoyed intermittent sunshine, appreciating the fact that after rain the atmosphere is crystal clear and lacking in the haziness which often accompanies hot weather.

Edith Olivier tells the story – in her *Wiltshire* (1951) – of the destitute man dying in a hospital in the East End of London. When asked by the doctor if he wanted anything he was heard to mutter: 'Yes, the Marlborough Downs in the rain'. Not you will notice in the sunshine, but 'in the rain'.

Of all the weathers of the Downs the worst without doubt occurs when at low temperatures the rain turns to sleet or hail which is driven into your face by short squalls. Such weather was accurately described by Jefferies as 'a swan-shot of hail', for sleet or hail driven by a strong wind can sting the cheeks quite painfully.

The poet Charles Sorley wrote of the Marlborough Downs as the place 'where the mists swim and the winds blow' and there certainly is a particular grandeur about them in rough weather when the wind rages and torments the beeches of the hilltop clumps. I have been on an exposed hillfort in conditions when I could hardly stand against a gale force wind, and found the experience extremely exhilarating. There is usually at least a slight breeze blowing across the Downs, which prompted Dean Farrar of Marlborough College in the nineteenth century to write of 'the free fresh downs with the winds of heaven that breathe health over them'.

The hilltop beech clumps demonstrate the extremes on these Downs, being wind-torn and occasionally uprooted by the strong winds which sometimes ravage them in their exposed situations. By contrast, in gentler weather they provide a serene element in the downland scene. Edward Thomas expressed these extremes beautifully when he wrote in *The South Country* (1909):

> The beeches on the beech-covered hills roar and strain as if they would fly off with the hill, and soon they are as meek as a great horse leaning his head over a gate.

At midsummer the heat of the Marlborough Downs in the sun can be intolerable, with few trees to provide shade. Sunlight tends to be harsh at midday, especially at midsummer, and these Downs are therefore better seen at morning or evening and preferably in spring or autumn when the sun is not at its zenith and is consequently casting long shadows which enhance the landscape. The Downs are particularly fine on a sunny day with a breeze, when shadows of the clouds go scurrying across the contoured downland.

The downs should also be experienced in their moodier days when mist or fog envelopes the hills. Such conditions add mystery to the landscape as normally familiar objects loom as blurred grey silhouettes out of the mist, and sounds are deadened by the all-embracing whiteness. The dramatic long views are lost, but are there for another day. Some of the remote and more mysterious archaeological sites – for example standing stones or the Devil's Den – are best visited on moody or misty days, as such weather adds to their air of mystery.

A fall of snow transforms the Downs from a normally benign landscape into a more bleak and threatening one. Well-known scenes look different under snow, the landscape becomes virtually monochrome, and features are revealed which are not seen in normal conditions. When snow is thawing it tends to linger in slight depressions, and ditches appear where there were apparently no ditches before. Consequently snow is a great aid to the discovery of previously unrecognised ancient ditches and field systems.

No account of landscape and climate should ignore the skies, particularly in the austere topography of the Marlborough Downs where the skies assume added importance arising from the simplicity and elemental character of the landscape. The wide expansive skies, ranging from a dull leaden grey overcast to a brilliant azure blue sometimes studded with white cloudlets, are a significant and dramatic feature of the downland scene.

W.H. Hudson wrote of Wiltshire downland in *A Shepherd's Life* (1909); 'all colours and sound have a purity and vividness and intensity beyond that in other places'. This wonderful clarity and carrying power of sound was well illustrated to me one day when resting on the knoll near the east end of Smeathe's Ridge. Although no one was in sight on the open down when I went to the knoll I soon became aware of human voices. Every word of the conversation was audible to me, and yet when I looked around to see how I had been so rapidly approached I was surprised to discover that the speakers were in close conversation about a quarter of a mile away. This phenomenon of sound carrying in downland applies to animal as well as human sounds, to the bleating of sheep, the lowing of cattle, and to bird song. It renders mechanical sounds of farm machinery, motor vehicles and aeroplanes particularly obtrusive, and must presumably be due to the extreme purity of the atmosphere.

Rivers and Winterbournes

Closely associated with climate and rainfall is the subject of water supply. Surface water is particularly scarce in the Marlborough Downs, and water for man and beast has always posed something of a problem in this area. We have seen that rainfall is moderate, and the only rivers are the Kennet and Og, together with their feeder streams. The head waters of these rivers are called 'winterbournes' because they are intermittent and tend to run only in winter. They give the names to villages such as Winterbourne Monkton and Winterbourne Bassett, and their inconsistency of flow has posed a problem to cartographers who show the winterbourne which runs through these two villages to feed the Kennet as a discontinuous line on the map.

Following the unusually dry winters of the late 1980s and early 1990s the water level in the River Kennet dropped alarmingly. For long periods the beds of both the river and its winterbournes were quite dry. This is not unusual in the winterbournes, but the diminution of the Kennet has understandably concerned many people. It has been alleged by some that the dearth of water is the consequence of increased extraction by the water authorities, and a society has been formed to protect the River Kennet.

The Kennet has two principal sources. The first is the winterbourne just mentioned, sometimes known as the Upper Kennet, which rises near Broad Hinton on Uffcott Down and flows south past Avebury to join the Kennet near Swallowhead Springs which provide the other source of the Kennet. At these springs the Kennet turns east and runs a little south of the the A4 at a level well above the floor of the parallel and dry Vale of Pewsey to its south, through the Kennett villages to Marlborough and the east (Why, I often wonder, is the river spelt with a single 't', and the villages with double 't'?).

A little north-east of Marlborough the Kennet is joined by its tributary the River Og – surely the shortest river name in England – sometimes known as the Ogbourne, which runs south as a winterbourne from its source near Ogbourne St. George through the Ogbourne villages. At Bay Bridge (187 710) the Og was dammed before 1204 to form the 'King's Great Stew', this being the fishpond for the occupants of Marlborough Castle a mile and a half to its south.

A very occasional winterbourne rises at Rockley where several wells were shown on the first series 1:25,000 map between Rockley and Old Eagle. This stream was known as the Hungerbourne or Hunger Brook from the belief that it rose every seven years and presaged calamity. The brook, which ran down the valley to join the Og at Bay Bridge, has diminished in recent years due to the lowering of the water table, but in particularly wet autumns the road at Old Eagle used to be flooded; in 1776 there was a proposal to change the route of the highway at Rockley because of the flooding (document in Wiltshire Record Office). Rockley Manor is situated on the course of the Hungerbourne and is said to have culverts incorporated in its cellars to conduct the water under the house when the winterbourne rises. In 1910-12 the stream constantly rose and in 1915 it formed several lakes in the grounds of Rockley Manor. There was an exceptional rising of the Hungerbourne in December 1960 which was said to have been the first since 1915, and it rose again in 1977.

Associated with the dearth of rivers in the Marlborough Downs is the consequential lack of fords. The Ridgeway formerly forded the Kennet (at 120 677) on its way south to East Kennett, but the only ford name within the Marlborough Downs is Clatford, where the track running south from Fyfield Down crossed the river by a ford (156 687) which may still be seen immediately east of the bridge. This route was one of Britton's second-class road in 1809. Another ford name is Axford at the very edge of the area under discussion.

Prehistoric man knew nothing of well-sinking and natural water sources were then of vital importance and as such were revered. The cult of water deities was widespread among Celtic peoples and many springs, river sources and ponds acquired a sanctity which was applied to holy wells in later times. It is perhaps relevant to note that a cluster of tumuli exist in a rather unusual low situation around the source of the Hungerbourne at Rockley, which may be an indication that the Bronze Age people revered the site of these springs which would then have been more active, the water table being then much higher. It is interesting to speculate whether the mystery over the immense effort expended in constructing Silbury Hill in the Neolithic period might be explained by its proximity to Swallowhead Springs where the winterbourne and the springs combine to form the effective joint source of the Kennet. In this context it is relevant to note that up to the mid-nineteenth century local people used to ascend Silbury Hill 'on every Palm Sunday, when they make merry with cakes, figs, sugar, and water fetched from the swallow head, or spring of the Kennet' (William Stukeley). These ceremonies may have been survivals from prehistoric ones at which the source of the Kennet was worshipped.

Wells

Having established the scarcity of rivers in the Marlborough Downs, in the many places where water was not naturally available recourse had to be made to digging wells or constructing dewponds. Wells were not known in pre-Roman times, and where later wells were dug in the Downs they often had to be excavated to considerable depths before water was reached.

A number of Roman 'wells' have been discovered between Silbury Hill – around which the Roman road diverted – and Swallowhead Springs. These were excavated to a depth of about twenty feet in solid chalk. Reverting to the possibility that this area around Silbury may have been the site of ritual connected with the joint source of the River Kennet, it is interesting to speculate whether these 'wells' could have been ritual shafts of the type described by Stuart Piggott in *The Druids* (1968). He tells us that 'Evidence from Eastern Europe shows us that such shafts have an ancestry going back to the middle of the second millennium B.C.' Such ritual shafts are not unknown in this country, and Professor Piggott also writes: 'These ritual shafts, some of which may have functioned at one time as wells, linked the Celtic cult of the underworld with that of springs and water'. It is possible that here the Romans converted existing prehistoric ritual shafts into wells for their travellers, or they may have continued to use them as they too made use of such votive offering shafts which often contain a great variety of gifts to the deity. These have been confused with wells because their tops were often constructed of vaulted masonry. In this situation near Swallowhead Springs these shafts may represent a long tradition of prehistoric ritual connected with worship of the joint Winterbourne and Swallowhead source of the River Kennet. Attention should perhaps be drawn to Mrs. N. Chadwick's references in her study of *The Celts* (1970) to Celtic ritual at 'watersides', their reverence for 'sacred lakes and rivers' and the sanctuaries which they created 'at the sources of the Marne and the Seine'.

Silbury and The Kennet

The established Neolithic origin of Silbury seems to prove that it was not sepulchral in purpose as the sepulchres of that age were long barrows and round barrows did not appear, so far as is known, until the later Bronze Age. It is significant that the two other very large man-made mounds in the district – the Mount at Marlborough and the former Hatfield Barrow at Marden which had been levelled by 1818 – were both associated with water, Marlborough Mount being in a wide bend of the River Kennet and Hatfield Barrow standing in a similar bend in the infant River Avon (092 583). Significantly neither of these mounds have yielded an interment, and according to Stukeley: 'There is a spring in the ditch' of Marlborough Mount. Its association with the magician Merlin is also interesting, as is Colt Hoare's conclusion that Hatfield Barrow 'May have been devoted to religious as well as civic purposes, either as a Hill Altar, or a locus consecratus'. This brings to mind the 'altar of earth' in the Book of Exodus (20, verse 24) which is very preoccupied with the importance of water and wells.

The bridge which has replaced the ford at East Kennett, looking north. On the slope in the background the Saxons intercepted the Danish host in AD 1006

Liddington Foilly (right) at the west end of Liddington Hill (left)

At the centre of Silbury Dean Merewether discovered in 1849 a carefully constructed small mound – which had later been enlarged into Silbury as we know it – associated with 'great quantities of moss' which evidently had come from some damp location. This moss survived, still green from Neolithic times over 5,000 years earlier – to be seen by Professor Atkinson during his televised exploration of Silbury Hill in 1967.

A further fact which suggests that the effort of constructing Silbury Hill was connected with the nearby sources of the River Kennet is to be found at Bath. Here the hot springs were dedicated to the Celtic goddess Sul. The town was Romanised to *Aquae Sulis*, and the goddess to Sul-Minerva. The goddess Sul was worshipped 'on the tops of hills overlooking springs' according to H. W. Scarth (*Aquae Sulis*, 1864), and near Bath we find Solsbury Hill, which formerly was *Sulsbury*. The Roman road to Bath passes between Silbury Hill and Swallowhead, and Silbury appears in the 1281 Assize Rolls as *Seleburgh*. A development from 'Sul' to 'Sele' over some twelve hundred years and to 'Sil' by 1663 seems eminently feasible, particularly as 'Sul', and 'Sil' are phonetically similar, and *The Place-Names of Wiltshire* frankly admits that: 'we have very little to go upon in the interpretation of the name [Silbury], and its meaning must remain as uncertain as the history of the hill itself'.

Another fact worth noting is that early writers drew attention to the relationship of Silbury Hill to the River Kennet. Leland in 1540-42 mentioned that: 'Kennet riseth at Selbiri hille bottom', and in the eighteenth century Stukeley wrote of: 'Silbury Hill, where the real Head of the Kennet is'. In wet winters water stands in the ditch around Silbury and, bearing in mind that in prehistoric times the water table was much higher, it seems probable that the ditch was intended to hold water and reflect the hill on its surface. Flinders-Petrie came to this conclusion in 1922 when he wrote: 'The low situation of Silbury Hill can only be due to the need to make a water fosse around it' (*WAM* 42).

Donkey Wheels

When in much later times wells were dug in upland areas they often had to be excavated to great depths to reach water, and were sometimes provided with a tread-wheel at the head to raise the water. Such wheels were often operated by a donkey or, it is said, a labourer when a donkey was not available, the water being lifted in a large bucket.

Such donkey wheels were large structures of timber usually about 4.2 metres in diameter and 900 millimetres wide. They were not unusual in this area and examples are known to have existed at Broad Hinton, Snap and Lower Upham. The Broad Hinton wheel was mentioned by Jefferies as being in part of a cottage and was dismantled in 1908, but an illustration of it survived and has been reproduced in a number of publications. The Snap wheel, which was also mentioned by Richard Jefferies, has now gone, but at Lower Upham the donkey-wheel survives disused in a farm building.

Windpumps

The deep wells with donkey-wheels tended to be replaced by boreholes with metal-vaned windpumps which survive in a number of places but all now disused. Derelict examples may be seen at Southend south of Ogbourne St. George, at Snap, Mudgell, Draycot Foliat, Lower Upham and Winterbourne Monkton. The last (at 104 725) was erected on the base of a former windmill. Snap is of interest because the donkey-wheel here (224 764) seems to have been replaced by the windpump which was in time replaced by the electric pump-house along the valley south of High Clear Plantation. Upper Upham is said never to have had its own water prior to the mains supply being laid on and to have been supplied by water cart from the well at Snap, and there is an old tradition that as long ago as the fourteenth century when John of Gaunt hunted from his lodge at Upper Upham he used to go to Aldbourne for his baths. There was also a tradition among local people that the village of Snap was abandoned as a result of the failure of its water-supply. This has generally been decried and does seem improbable, although I have been told by an elderly lady in Swindon that in about 1917 a civil engineer friend of her father's called Cyril Thomas was employed to sink a well at Snap, but his search for water failed.

Dewponds

The alternative to wells as a source of water in upland areas was the dewpond. These ponds, which were constructed from early times, were generally circular and were constructed by specialist gangs up to the Second World War. Their construction was complicated and their name may be a misnomer as it is problematical how much of their water was obtained from dew as opposed to rainfall, but they were common on the Downs and examples are often seen, now usually dry. Kipling described a Sussex '... dewpond on the height, Unfed, that never fails', and Richard Jefferies, after sampling the water of many Wiltshire dewponds, pronounced that their water has a 'dead flavour'. The most celebrated dewpond in the Marlborough Downs is Oxenmere – in Anglo-Saxon *Oxnamere* – which is known to be at least eleven hundred years old and still holds water.

Oxenmere on Milk Hill, mentioned in Anglo-Saxon charters and reputed to be the oldest dewpond in England.

The problem of how hillforts on their waterless summits were provided with the water that enabled them to withstand seige has exercised the minds of archaeologists for many years. The usual conclusion is that their occupants constructed dewponds, but I am by no means convinced that they had acquired that knowledge and so far as I know no authenticated examples of Iron Age dewponds have been discovered. It seems likely that rainwater was collected, and this suggestion gains credence from Sir Mortimer Wheeler's 1934-7 excavation of Maiden Castle hillfort in Dorset. His report reveals that some of the pits at Maiden Castle contained water butts fed by ditches which discharged into them. The Department of the Environment official handbook to Maiden Castle described these pits as 'sumps or water-containers'.

The shepherd and his family who lived on the summit of Martinsell had to rely on a pond for water, as did the occupant of the ruined cottage at Old Totterdown on the line of the droveway which ran from Glory Ann Pond to Marlborough. Such hilltop ponds were of immense importance to drovers on these arid heights because their cattle demanded frequent watering, and dewponds tend to appear at regular intervals along drove routes, as for example on the droveway from Tan Hill over Knap Hill and past Martinsell which has ponds at Oxenmere, Golden Ball Hill, Draycot Hill, Huish Hill, Oare Hill, and Martinsell Hill (174 636) at intervals of generally less than a mile. When William Cobbett came to the Marlborough Downs on one of his *Rural Rides* he had the following to say about ponds in his entry for 6 November 1821:

> Marlborough ... is succeeded, on my route to Swindon, by an extensive and very beautiful down about four miles over. Here nature has flung the earth about in a great variety of shapes. The fine short smooth grass has about 9 inches of mould under it, and then comes the chalk. The water that runs down the narrow side-hill valleys is caught, in different parts of the down, in basins made on purpose and lined with clay apparently. This is for watering the sheep in summer, sure sign of a really dry soil; and yet the grass never parches on these downs. The chalk holds the moisture, and the grass is fed by the dews in hot and dry weather. At the end of this down the high country ends.

As cattle began to be introduced on to the high downland in the mid-nineteenth century it became evident that the dewponds could not satisfy their need for water which is greater than that of sheep. In *Wildlife in a Southern County* (1879) Jefferies described 'the immense labour of watering cattle on the hills' and how in a dry summer 'all day long files of water-carts go down into the hollows where the springs burst forth, and at such times half the work of the farm consists in fetching the precious liquid perhaps a mile or more.'

Piped Water

After the Great War of 1914-1918 the downland farmers, having found the dewponds inadequate to water their cattle which were increasingly being grazed on the Downs, and having tired of the expense and effort of carting water to the hills, instigated schemes for piped water. In 1931 Smeathe's Ridge was supplied, as was the east flank of Walker's Hill. Such schemes were progressively introduced to most of the Downs using reservoirs to hold the water which was then gravity fed to the dispersed cattle troughs. Such reservoirs may be seen all over the Marlborough Downs, at for example Temple Bottom (142 726), west of Snap (212 765) and around Ogbourne St. George.

Today the water for Swindon is extracted from boreholes on Whitefield Hill between Ogbourne St. George and Snap, and is then piped to a reservoir south-east of Wroughton.

Woods

The general character of the Marlborough Downs is that of open grassland. The thin topsoil does not normally generate much growth of trees although woods do grow, especially where the clay-with-flints overlays the chalk. The largest of these woods is West Woods which is an outlier of Savernake Forest on the clay-with-flints a little south-west of Marlborough.

On Fyfield Down north-east of Avebury Totterdown Woods – once again on clay-with-flints – is old woodland containing introduced rhododendron which is a wildlife refuge on these high downs. Nearby Wroughton Copse (138 709) is more ancient woodland formerly associated with the twelfth century settlement, but Delling Copse (132 711) is a modern copse containing many Scots pine probably created as a game covert in the nineteenth century when this area was part of a shooting estate owned by the Meux family. Wroughton Copse has nothing to do with Wroughton, being a corruption of 'Raddun', but towards Wroughton village is more old woodland in a narrow coombe called Clouts Wood. There is also a scatter of woodland including Chase Woods east of Ogbourne St. George towards Aldbourne in Aldbourne Chase, and strips of woodland embower the isolated village of Rockley at the very heart of the Downs. Shelter belts of beech also occur, for example the belt which crosses the Broad Hinton to Marlborough road north-west of Rockley.

Beech Clumps

The hilltop clumps of trees are normally eighteenth or early-nineteenth century plantings as landscape features. They resemble islands in the ocean of the Downs. Such clumps are Four Mile Clump – really a small wood – on the turnpike road four miles out of Marlborough and associated with the poet Sorley, the three beech clumps which adorn Hackpen Hill and are a landmark for miles around, Liddington Folly at the west end of Liddington Hill, and Liddington Clump at its east end. Clumps of trees planted for no apparent reason sometimes became known as follies. These hilltop clumps are a distinctive feature of the Marlborough Downs. They are planted not natural, but they positively embellish the landscape and I fear for their future when as at present they attain their maturity and show signs of decline. Some tree planting is occasionally still undertaken on the high Downs, as for example that on the Ridgeway above Lower Upham. Generally we do not now plant trees for posterity as did our ancestors, (although in eight days in 1991 35,000 trees were planted at Temple Farm, Rockley, using a newly invented Austrian tree-planting machine). Hilltop planting should be undertaken in a controlled way, for a clump of trees planted in a prominent position on a hill alters the landscape for generations to come. It goes without saying that such plantings should in all cases make use of indigenous trees.

On the exposed heights of the Marlborough Downs trees are frequently stunted or deformed from exposure to extreme winds. The 'wind-warped upland thorn' (Hardy) around which the Battle of Ashdown was fought in AD 868 a little to the east of the Marlborough Downs comes to mind. There are also the wind-harassed beech clumps on Liddington Hill, the Scots pine apparently killed and flayed of their bark by exposure on the south ramparts of Martinsell, and the deformed and stunted beeches on the east rampart of the same hill. Trees in such exposed situations often lean permanently with the prevailing wind and even in the comparative shelter of the Kennet Valley it is noticeable that since the excessive winds of 1989 and 1990 the trees between Fyfield and Manton have developed a distinct lean to the east away from the prevailing wind.

The three beech clumps on Hackpen Hill, one of the most prominent landmarks of the Marlborough Downs, seen from Winterbourne Bassett.

Trees

Richard Jefferies suggested that where there are beech the countryside is invariably beautiful, and the predominant tree of these Downs is the beech. An enigma about the beech is the fact that Aubrey recorded in 1685 that the only beech then existing in Wiltshire were in Grovely Wood towards the south of the county. This surprising statement about the tree which is generally assumed to be indigenous to the Downs is supported by Thomas Davis who wrote late in the eighteenth century: 'Beech timber is not common in the county'. The evidence suggests that the beech was uncommon in Wiltshire until it was extensively planted in the late eighteenth and nineteenth centuries, and that it is introduced rather than native. This suggestion is supported by Grose who wrote in *The Flora of Wiltshire*: 'the great bulk of beech wood in the county is of artificial origin dating from the early years of the nineteenth century'. Beech trees are shallow-rooted and relish lime, and consequently flourish on chalk capped with a thin bed of clay, as at Delling on Fyfield Down where a mature circle of beeches exists (136 714) beside the cottage within the former rabbit warren. One of the early signs of spring is for me the tawny wine-red hue assumed by beech trees as their buds begin to swell and lengthen, to be succeeded in due time by the exceptionally fresh green of the translucent young foliage.

Small clumps or rows of Scots pine are to be seen on the Marlborough Downs used as markers to define routes and establishments frequented by drovers. An example of a pine-line droveway may be seen running east from Barbury over Burderop Down, and at 'Dane Barn' (Andrews and Dury's name at 126 738) beside the Ridgeway on Hackpen Hill we have a barn surrounded with Scots pine which may have been a 'stance' or overnight stopping-place for drovers and their animals.' ('stance' presumably derives from the verb to stand). It is a fact that the Waggon and Horses at Beckhampton was built in 1669 as The Bear Inn with adjoining drove-closes to accommodate droves, and this inn is marked by Scots pine at its west gable. Scots pine are, like beech, normally a planted rather than a native species in the south of England.

Another introduced species which has been grown in Britain for several hundred years is the larch, which is a deciduous conifer. Larches are occasionally seen in this area, at for example the large copse at Upper Herdswick on the turnpike road at the east end of Barbury Castle car park. Yew trees are unusual in the Marlborough Downs except planted in churchyards and occasionally along old traffic routes; there are a few on Oare and Huish Hills. Box trees survive in the cottage gardens of the deserted village of Snap, having developed from former box hedging and holly appears in hedgerows all over these Downs, as does the crab apple. Of deciduous trees hornbeam appear occasionally, for example the group east of Snap at the south edge of High Clear Plantation on the valley track from Snap to Aldbourne, and they also occur at Rockley. Hornbeam are almost certainly always planted. The common deciduous trees such as whitebeam, field maple, crab, wayfaring tree, aspen, ash, lime and both species of chestnut are to be seen in the area. Horse chestnuts line the B4192 road at Shipley Bottom where they are said to have been planted by Lady Curry of Upper Upham. They also line the droveway which runs north-east from Ogbourne Maizey, and are to be seen in numbers along the river at East Kennett. Lime trees may be seen at Rockley but oak is infrequent on the chalk, although it occurs for example in Chase Woods on Round Hill Downs, and it is numerous on Clench Common towards

Martinsell. Birch is occasionally seen, again at Clench Common, and though not native sycamore spreads vigorously on the chalk. Hawthorn, blackthorn and elder are common in the woodlands and hedgerows of the area, as is hazel which often survives in copses which once were coppiced but have now run wild. These coppices are often found near the upland villages such as Snap (for example at 221 763); it is a shame that the coppicing craft is not revived for there exists a demand for hazel for thatching spars, woven hurdles for garden use, and for walking sticks. The revival of some of these coppices would also be of great benefit to wildlife. Of smaller shrubs gorse is not uncommon despite the fact that Grose suggests that it avoids the chalk, but juniper is, to use the words of Grose, 'almost absent from the northern [Wiltshire] chalk'.

The alien Lombardy poplar is not often seen in downland country and is unusual in this area, although in the 1970s a row of Lombardy poplars was planted along the road from Ogbourne Maizey to Old Eagle. Many of these are now growing well. Some people dislike this tree, but I am rather fond of its emphatic exclamation-like impact in the landscape. It is however in my view best planted as a single specimen or in a small group, rather than in the formal Gallic manner in lines beside roads as here near Old Eagle.

In some places – notably between Chase Woods and Southend – the English elm is regenerating to some size from suckers following the Dutch elm disease, but presumably the disease will strike again when the trees are more mature. There were formerly many dead elms at Snap which stood for long white and flayed of their bark and, resembling skeletons and added to the desolation of the deserted village, but these have now been cleared away and extensive tree planting has taken place.

Wild Flowers

The subject of the wild flowers of the Marlborough Downs is a considerable one and I am no botanist, but an imperfect knowledge of botany does not necessarily imply a lack of appreciation of the beauty of wild flowers and the notes that follow are written from an aesthetic rather than a botanical standpoint. They do not pretend to be a comprehensive account of the wild flora of the Marlborough Downs, and rely to a great extent on others who were more knowledgeable in the subject than myself.

Some parts of these calcareous grasslands are very rich in downland species, in particular the area around Glory Ann and Totterdown east of the Ridgeway on Hackpen Hill, and also the area around Knap and Walker's Hills at the southern edge of these Downs. Grose suggests that: 'the chalk downs to the north [of the Kennet and Avon Canal] are in general of little interest, but the magnificent range of hills from Martinsell to Easton overlooking the Vale of Pewsey bears the chalkland species in abundance.' Walker's Hill in particular is well worth an early summer visit, for most downland flowers are at their best in May and June. The survival mechanism of many of the downland species is to grow and bloom very close to the earth, in order that they can set seed and propagate themselves despite the attentions of grazing sheep.

The wild flower which immediately comes to mind in connection with the Marlborough Downs is the ubiquitous meadow cranesbill of the long grass verges, the favourite flower of Richard Jefferies. Many wild orchids are to be found on the north-facing banks of the Workway Drove as it crosses the south shoulder of Knap Hill, and the similar bank of the Ridgeway north of Barbury Castle. There is a profusion of the blue chalk milkwort to be seen on Knap and Walker's Hills, and the yellow *helianthemum* (or rock-rose) is said to have given Golden Ball its name, although the name could equally well originate from the multitude of cowslips which appear on these hills in advance of the *helianthemum* flowers. Milkwort is an interesting species in that it is abundant, it ranges in colour from deep blue through pale blue to white, and is in some places pink, red and purple, but the colour variations do not seem normally to occur together. This suggests that the variation may be due to the soil conditions. The herbalist Gerard listed six types of milkwort, and in his day it was believed that cattle which ate milkwort would give more milk.

The downland scarp of Milk Hill, Walker's Hill and Knap Hill was in 1968 leased from New College Oxford by the Nature Conservancy Council as the Pewsey Downs National Nature Reserve, principally as a result of its rich flora and the associated insect fauna. This open grassland with its diversity of flowering plants has been created by man's use of the area since prehistoric times for grazing his animals, and for the last hundred years this land has been farmed by the Stratton family. This century its traditional use as a sheepwalk has – as in other parts of the Marlborough

Downs – been changed to mixed grazing with cattle taking their turn with the sheep. If the turf is left ungrazed coarse grasses and scrub take over as may be seen on the lower slopes of Knap Hill, but the introduction of cattle poses problems. The larger animals can cause erosion on steep slopes and there is also the problem that by poaching the ground cattle may encourage the spread of plants such as thistle and ragwort which thrive on disturbed ground. Ragwort when it wilts becomes poisonous to cattle and has to be cleared where cattle graze. Another problem associated with cattle is the danger of introducing unwanted alien plants when hay is brought in as feed.

The only Wiltshire locations given by John Gooders in *A Day in the Country* (1979) are both in the Marlborough Downs. First he mentions the Pewsey Down reserve which he describes as 'one of the finest pieces of downland remaining in Britain'. The flowers which he lists for this area are orchids – including the burnt-tip – eyebright, rock-rose, chalk milkwort, harebell, round-headed campion, early gentian, bastard toadflax, snakeshead fritillary – which must surely be a mistake – and others. The other area of Wiltshire mentioned by Gooders is the Fyfield Down Nature Reserve, for which he mentions early gentian, chalk milkwort, and frog orchid.

These grasslands grow grasses in infinite variety, together with scabious, harebell, horse-shoe vetch and bird's foot trefoil, and multitudes of other species which encourage butterflies to proliferate on the rich flora. Bird's foot trefoil was the first wild flower which the young Richard Jefferies learned to identify, although he knew it as the bird's foot lotus. Silverweed and pineapple mayweed pave the Ridgeway along Hackpen Hill, and bluebells carpet the floor of woods such as West Woods in spring, together with primrose, pink campion and stitchwort. Broom rape is occasionally seen in the long grass verges of downland trackways, particularly in the Ogbourne area. A profuse mixture of rose-bay willow herb and blackberries lines the Ridgeway path as it passes Chase Woods above the Ogbournes, and rest-harrow is seen in places, for example on the descent of Green Street from the Ridgeway to Avebury. Thistles in great variety and numbers appear, often accompanied by knapweed with its purple flowers, on for example Overton Down. Recently the proliferation of speedwell seems to be making this one of the most common of wild flowers of the Marlborough Downs.

The strong stems of the wild clematis, or traveller's joy, swarm over the hedges and cover them with the fluff of 'old man's beard' in autumn. The stems of wild clematis were used in the past by shepherds to repair their hurdles, and I know of a case in Gloucestershire where it was used to bind the undercoat of thatch to rafters. The shepherds called it 'Devil's Guts' because it was so very tough. Another climber which ranges through the hedgerows is the honeysuckle, and convolvulus runs riot in some areas in late summer with its attractive white and pink blossoms. The wild clematis also appears in chalk-pits where the flower communities tend to differ from those of the open downland, and often produce surprises.

Sometimes it is a detail of the scene which epitomises a landscape. This may be man-made – for example a standing stone erected perhaps as long ago as Neolithic times. It may be a natural element such as a tiny wild flower nesting in the crevice of a sarsen stone, or a splodge of lichen on that same stone. Such lichens grow in great variety on sarsen stones, particularly on those of Overton and Fyfield Downs. The poet George Grabbe, who was rector of Trowbridge and was interested in geology, wrote of:

> 'The living stains, which Nature's hand alone,
> Profuse of life, pours out upon the stones...'

The lichens make this area of particular interest, as do the species of flowers which grow in the localised acidification caused by the rainfall run off from the sandstone of the sarsens, which are distinct from the normal chalk grassland species.

The yellow-flowered ragwort displays the ragged leaves which give it its name on disturbed ground such as rabbit warrens or areas grazed by cattle, and yellow toadflax is common in the Marlborough Downs. The Wiltshire names for this flower include 'butter and eggs' or 'eggs and bacon'; Jefferies refers to toadflax as 'butter and eggs' in *Round about a Great Estate*, where he mentions that in the woods it is often pale, but 'upon the Downs it is a deep and beautiful yellow'.

Violets are profuse on the chalk of this district. In 1991 a mass of white violets appeared on a hedgebank near the former railway bridge at Southend near Ogbourne St. George. Of the beautiful wood anemone –

which he calls the 'wind anemone' – Richard Jefferies warns 'how easy it is to miss their fleeting loveliness'. The prostrate and creeping wild thyme carpets areas of short grass in places and is frequently seen on the anthills of unimproved grassland. On the Downs thyme occurs most widely on the superficial deposits overlaying the chalk. Jefferies noted that it 'calls up a vision of the Downs', and mentions it growing 'on the noble slopes of the hills, and along the sward-grown fosse of ancient earthworks'.

I have had the five-flowered 'town hall clock' (or moschatel) pointed out to me at Snap, and have chanced upon salad burnet on Wansdyke. The latter is often seen in areas frequented by rabbits because, like *helianthemum* and thyme, it can withstand close grazing. Aubrey noted 'The turfe (at Avebury) rich and fragrant with thyme and burnet'. When crushed salad burnet gives off the scent of cucumber, which led to it being used in salads.

Now that less weedkillers are being used red poppies often appear along field margins and sprinkle the corn. They were common in the time of Jefferies and he called them the 'lords of the July fields'.

Edward Thomas, who was in the habit of listing place-names, also lists the flowers of the Marlborough Downs in his biography of Richard Jefferies. First he mentions 'the chalk-land flowers – hop, trefoil, saw-wort, scabious, purple gentian and poppy', together with 'harebells, sweet basil, and trefoil' Then: 'On Barbury Hill we are among harebell, rock-rose, scabious and trefoil blossoms'. Hackpen Hill he describes as 'paving itself with harebell, silverweed, eyebright and bartsia'. Referring to Richard Jefferies on Liddington Hill, Thomas rather overdid the flowers: 'As he took deep breaths of air about its harebell, eyebright, clover, bedstraw, scabious and fine grass, his brain was furrowed and sown with the thoughts that became *The Story of My Heart*.' Also writing of Liddington and Richard Jefferies Geoffrey Grigson, who lived at nearby Broad Town and wrote *The Englishman's Flora* (1955) and the *Dictionary of English Plant Names* (1974), mentioned that; 'a small uncommon pretty bright yellow flower, the field flea-wort, grows there as if in his memory'.

Wild hops are occasionally found as climbers in hedgerows beside the downland tracks. Some are to be found on the west escarpment of the hills on the Ridgeway overlooking Lower Upham. Here they are near the site of the Roman pavement mentioned by Jefferies. Pliny mentions the hop as a garden plant of the Romans; they are known to have used the hop as we eat asparagus utilising the fresh shoots and although the hop is said to have been introduced in about 1525 AD when it was taken into cultivation, it was probably native in its wild state. Elsewhere in these Downs, the villagers of Aldbourne used to collect wild hops from Stock Lane – the lane which follows a straight line from Marlborough to Aldbourne – to use in their beer-making.

Birds

The restricted amount of woodland and the scarcity of water in the Marlborough Downs tend to conspire against birds and mammals, and yet the number of species is not as limited as might be expected in these circumstances. As is to be expected the skylark is much in evidence on the Downs and is usually regarded as the bird which epitomises the downland, but I would make a case for the corn-bunting with his coarse jangling cry as the bird which for me typifies these Downs. Pairs of corn-buntings used to be limited to the northern end of the Marlborough Downs around Barbury Castle, but of recent years they have extended southwards and their unmusical but distinctive calls are to be heard in many places in these Downs at many seasons of the year. Very occasionally wheatear are seen, but the ploughing of the high downs has greatly reduced their numbers. Many lapwing – I prefer their alternative name of peewit – are seen, first as agitated parents performing aerial acrobatics in the spring, and then again in often vast numbers when they flock in the autumn. The green woodpecker is often heard, but not so often seen, 'yaffling' in the woods on Fyfield Down.

Buzzards are infrequently seen in the Marlborough Downs except around Martinsell towards Savernake Forest. Their presence on Fyfield Down was recorded in the Natural History Section of *WAM* 58, and there are records of the rabbit keepers on the Fyfield Down Warren tolerating the buzzards because they scavenged the dead rabbits – and were believed never to take live ones! Nearby Pickledean (140 691) derives its name from an Old English word meaning 'hawk-valley'.

Other birds of prey sometimes seen include kestrels and an occasional hobby. Fyfield Down provides a winter refuge for short-eared owls, but the barn owl is now very rare despite the fact that some farmers place owl boxes in their open barns on these Downs. Swallows and house-martins may often be seen hawking for insects low over the racehorse gallops. Yellow-hammers sing from the downland bushes, and meadow-pipits frequently perch on the standing stones in the Downs. The chiff-chaff, which is so longed-for as a harbinger of spring, sings his repetitive call in the high trees but becomes progressively more boring as he persists in singing it interminably throughout the summer.

Warblers are commonly seen in the wayside hedges of thorn and elder in spring and summer, and large mixed flocks of redwing and fieldfare forage in the bigger trees on migration in spring and autumn. Starlings often associate with flocks of sheep, as do jackdaws, crows, and rooks. The village of Rockley derives its name from 'Rooks leah' meaning rooks' clearing, and rooks remain much in evidence there. Rooks also nest in the Hackpen beech clumps. Many chaffinches are present in these Downs, and cuckoos are sometimes seen.

Mammals

Of the large mammals park deer – that is fallow deer – were formerly common in Aldbourne Chase and were enclosed in a number of deer parks. John Aubrey was hunting deer 'at large' in these Downs when he discovered Avebury in the seventeenth century. Roe and muntjac deer are frequently seen, generally singly or in very small groups, but fallow deer are now not so often seen. 'Beware of deer' traffic signs near Wansdyke on the Alton to Lockeridge minor road confirm the existence of deer in this area, which is near Savernake. I have often seen them here, as I have also seen an alarmed roebuck on the A345 at Southend near Ogbourne St. George.

Although wild deer may be chanced upon practically anywhere in these Downs, they are most likely to be seen in one of the many little frequented coombes that are enclosed by banks of down, These – of which examples are Shipley Bottom and the unnamed combe (153 753) south of Barbury Castle both of which are crossed by public footpaths – the deer regard as secure refuge in a landscape which is deficient in tree cover.

There is much evidence of badgers on these hills, particularly on the Ridgeway and Wansdyke, but these persecuted and nocturnal animals are seldom seen except as casualties on the roads. Foxes are occasionally seen;

early one Sunday morning, before most people were about, I once saw a fox on the eastern bank at Avebury. There is a considerable fox problem at Levett's Poultry Farm a mile north of Martinsell. I have already described how rabbits were formerly farmed in warrens. The extent of these former warrens emphasises the suitability of the terrain of these Downs as a habitat for rabbits which remain plentiful in the wild. On any visit to these Downs you may expect to see rabbits and a hare or two, but you are less likely to see deer or a fox. Stoats and weasels are seldom seen.

The grassland and arable of the Marlborough Downs also supports a considerable population of small mammals which are exploited by the birds of prey, and moles turn up their molehills – known locally as 'oont heaves' in former times. At Snap they sometimes turn up fragments of Victorian china, just as on Knap Hill they bring up pieces of seventeenth century clay pipes.

Farm Stock

Farm animals have much more impact on landscape than wild animals since they are present in greater numbers and make no attempt to conceal themselves. From Neolithic times the Marlborough Downs were used as sheepwalks and today sheep of various breeds remain the most common farm livestock. Very occasionally a flock of the old Wiltshire horn breed may be seen, usually beside Wansdyke or on the nearby escarpment overlooking Pewsey Vale. This breed almost died out and remains very rare, although in former times it was the universal breed of sheep in these Downs before the breeds were improved. A distinctive feature of the Wiltshire horn is that it is a leggy sheep which sheds its wool and does not need to be sheared. Consequently its wool often hangs loose, but the most distinctive feature is the fact that both rams and ewes have horns. The lambs begin to sprout their horns at an early age and as a result take on a peculiarly demoniacal appearance when their horns first sprout. In his *General Agriculture of the County of Wilts* (1811), Thomas Davis stated that 'The sheep of this district may indeed be called the basis of Wiltshire Down husbandry', but the density of sheep on the Marlborough Downs is now greatly reduced.

Almost as rare an experience as seeing a flock of Wiltshire horn sheep is that of hearing sheep bells. I have heard these on a few occasions, but only once in the Marlborough Downs. That was in 1989 beside Wansdyke near the deserted village of Shaw, which was probably abandoned to make way for sheep. The evocative dull clunk of sheep bells, which are seamed and consequently do not ring, would once have been heard throughout these Downs.

'Land of sheep and sarsens' (Grigson): Wethers (sheep) and 'grey wethers' (sarsens) near Old Totterdown Woods (background).

Sheep in downland enhance the scene, but cattle are to me an anomaly on the downs from an aesthetic point of view. They have now to some extent supplanted sheep, and until a few years ago a herd of Highland longhorns were kept on Fyfield Down near Delling, but much more usual in the Marlborough Downs are the 'black and white' breeds.

The old grassland of the Downs – usually known as 'unimproved grassland' – is a particular type of turf which results from sheep grazing allowing rich plant communities to grow on thin infertile soils manured only by sheep dung. Geoffrey Grigson emphasised that it was grazing by sheep which created our downlands, pointing out that they would have existed geologically but that it was the sheep which produced the sward which was so fine that Stukeley likened the Wiltshire Downs to a 'Turkey Carpet'. Old grassland which has never been ploughed is often recognised by anthills. It has often been noticed that man-made earthworks have a particularly rich flora, and the same applies to anthills which are to be seen in profusion between the sarsen stones which prevented ploughing on Fyfield and Overton Downs.

These unimproved grasslands have been subjected to a regime of both grazing and the restriction of scrub growth. Light scrub, consisting of species such as hazel, hawthorn and elder, provides ideal habitat for many birds and other forms of wildlife, but if not controlled it becomes rife and impenetrable and its value to wildlife diminishes. Winter grazing is of especial importance to downland turf for it breaks down matted growth which would inhibit small plants from flowering and setting seed for the following year. The density of sheep upon a down is also important. Low density stocking allows the natural flora to flourish, but high density can poach the ground and leave bare patches which may be colonised by ragwort and other intruders.

The quality of downland turf is not entirely attributable to grazing by sheep. Mr J.D. Grose recorded in 1957 how in July 1954 the rabbit disease myxomatosis entered Wiltshire from the north. The epidemic was so virulent that by the end of 1954 the rabbit was practically eliminated from the Downs. With their abolition the downland flora underwent an astonishing transformation. The Downs began to resemble hayfields as the former short grasses grew to knee height, taller flowers flourished, and colonies of thistles appeared. The coarser grassland then declined further as scrub developed as a consequence of lack of grazing. This scrub has tended to survive even now that the rabbits have recovered some of their former density on the Downs.

The valuable racehorses which are trained in the Marlborough Downs are kept in the yards of their trainers and are seldom seen except on exercise, although mares with their foals are sometimes seen at for example Mudgell and Ogbourne Maizey. Pigs are seldom seen, although they are farmed in the open towards Calne, which was once a centre for the pig meat industry and about Rabley Wood east of Marlborough. If they are farmed elsewhere in the Marlborough Downs they must be in enclosed piggeries, like those which survive at Upper Upham Farm but appear to have been unoccupied for some years. In Victorian times, before the advent of the health inspector, the cottage pig was an essential element in the cottage economy at places such as Snap. During its last days in about 1907, after the cottagers had departed, Snap Farm became for a time a chicken farm run by an American college graduate who supplied London hotels with poultry, and today a large free-run chicken farm is run by Mr. Martin Pitt at Levett's Farm on Clench Common two miles south-west of Marlborough.

The current fashion for farming fallow deer has not yet been introduced into the Marlborough Downs, but it may well come for venison is very low in fat and accords with modern demand for low-fat meat. With regard to more exotic animals, I have not yet in this area had the startling experience which I once had in another part of Wiltshire when I chanced upon a pair of bison peacefully but incongruously grazing in a Wiltshire landscape! There is now a move to farm ostrich in England for meat, feathers, leather, and huge eggs of which I understand one will suffice for an omelette.

The Workway Drove descending into the Vale of Pewsey over the south flank of Knap Hill

6 Communications

The Wiltshire writer Geoffrey Grigson wrote:

> Roads, lanes, paths – we use them without reflecting how they are some of man's oldest inscriptions upon the landscape, how they are evidence of the wedding between men and their environment.

Prehistoric Tracks

From earliest times man and his beasts beat out the prehistoric tracks which criss-cross the downland in which they lived. In the Marlborough Downs the most celebrated of these tracks is the Ridgeway, which climbs north out of the Vale of Pewsey and passes over the col between Walker's Hill and Knap Hill. It cannot be proved to be prehistoric in origin, but the incidence of prehistoric monuments along its route suggest that this was the case, and prompted J.R.L. Anderson to entitle the best book on the Ridgeway *The Oldest Road;An Exploration of the Ridgeway*. From Pewsey Vale the Ridgeway runs north over Overton Hill and along Hackpen Hill where it swings north-east and runs from Barbury Castle across the head of the Og Valley past Liddington Hill and on into Berkshire, now Oxfordshire. In order to avoid the low-lying land of the Og Valley the Countryside Commission has for its Ridgeway long distance trail adopted a diversion from the true line of the Ridgeway from Barbury, down Smeathe's Ridge, through Southend, and then north past Chase Woods and over Round Hill Downs, rejoining the direct line of the Ridgeway near Liddington Hill.

From the Ridgeway near Glory Ann on Hackpen Hill (at 126 725) the top terrace of Silbury Hill can be seen peeping over the top of Waden Hill. Seen from this position, Silbury looks like a gentle long mound on the top of Waden Hill and there is no hint of the vast man-made mound which is concealed by the hill. It is interesting to speculate whether this is mere coincidence or deliberate, and whether it is possible that beacon fires were lighted on the flat top of Silbury to guide travellers from the east advancing along the Ridgeway down to Avebury. It is a fact that the old track from the Ridgeway near Glory Ann to Avebury – which was re-routed in the 1970s – descended Monkton Down among sarsens and tumuli very near a straight line drawn from Glory Ann to Silbury Hill.

The Roman burials which have been found beside the Ridgeway suggest that the old track continued to be used in Romano-British times, and it is significant that the Saxon battles which took place in the area were all associated with the Ridgeway which provided one of the principal routes by which armies of the period could move rapidly across the Downs.

Roman Roads

Two Roman roads crossed the Marlborough Downs. One ran east to west from Mildenhall (*Cunetio*) east of Marlborough, along the Kennet Valley where in some light conditions its agger may still be seen crossing the Ridgeway (119 683) a little north of the A4 at Overton Hill. It then looped around Silbury Hill – which may have been used as one of its sighting points – before continuing west out of the Marlborough Downs to Sandy Lane (*Verlucio*) near Calne. The other Roman road ran south from Wanborough on Ermin Way, where there was a Roman settlement, and followed the Og Valley through Ogbourne St. George to Mildenhall. A section of this road, now under tarmacadam, may be seen diverging from the A345 at Ogbourne St. George and climbing the hill, crossing the Countryside Commission's Ridgeway (at 205 734).

Saxon Way

An old Saxon way known as the Thieves' Way runs west to east through Shipley Bottom (223 784). Its Saxon name was *Scocera Weg*, and its name probably derives from its being used as a droveway for stolen cattle. Its age is indicated both by the fact that its route is marked by tumuli and by its coinciding with the parish boundary between Wanborough and Aldbourne. After leaving Shipley Bottom the Thieves' Way climbs the west flank of Sugar Hill and at the top crosses the Sugar Way, which runs along the crest of the hill, at a point known to the Saxons as *Red Stan* (Red

Stone). Sugar Way and Sugar Hill probably derive their names from Segur, a twelfth century landowner in Wanborough parish. Grundy, who solved many Anglo Saxon Charters, confused Sugar Way and Thieves' Way and was presumably responsible for the latter being incorrectly marked 'Sugar Way' on the 6-inch map.

Sugar Hill from Shipley Bottom to its west

Medieval Ways

Throughout the Medieval period the ridgeways, the other downland tracks and the Roman roads continued to be used by travellers and by drovers driving their herds and flocks across the countryside. No new roads were engineered until the coming of the turnpikes in the late seventeenth and eighteenth centuries. At these times, before the creation of definable roads and the coming of enclosure, it was quite usual to travel across country. Men on foot or riding horses across the Downs would sometimes take a distant mark and make straight for it, and this may explain the frequency with which tracks and footpaths are aligned on objects such as church towers or spires. Today with our road systems and signposts many people have lost that sense of direction which enabled our ancestors to travel across country, although it is retained by some habitual walkers and horse-riders in whom it is sometimes so instinctive that they hardly recognise its existence.

When it becomes wet chalk is sufficiently malleable to be displaced by traffic both animal and wheeled. Old traffic ways in downland tend to remain visible long after they have been abandoned. Where such ways climbed hills the chalk tended to be worked into corrugations as traffic ploughed the surface into a morass and then sought alternative ways up the hill. Examples are the fan-shaped pattern of ruts known as The Gangway (131 709) where the Old London Road climbed Overton Down beside Delling Copse, the parallel grooves where an old droveway from Shipley Bottom crossed the north end of Sugar Hill (227 797) on its way to join the Ridgeway at Fox Hill, and the similar traffic ruts where the Medieval way crossed the north-west flank of Knap Hill (121 637) above the Vale of Pewsey. Where traffic climbed diagonally or followed the contours along a slope shelf tracks tended to be formed as the wet chalk and the thin topsoil was displaced down the slope to form a counterscarp at the lower edge of the way, leaving the road upon a shelf. Continual traffic over a long period sometimes converted that shelf into a hollow-way, the counterscarp becoming so pronounced that the track was left in a hollow. Examples may be seen at the east end of Smeathe's Ridge (184 747) on the descent to Ogbourne St. George and at the old way which runs out of the Vale of Pewsey over the flank of Clifford's Hill near Rybury Camp (at 082 640) on its way to Tan Hill Fair site and on to Beckhampton. One of the interesting features of some of these old ways, best seen on Overton Down, is the way in which, despite the fact that they have been long abandoned, the grass on them retains a finer texture than the grass beside the tracks.

The long grassy descent eastwards from Upper Upham to New Barn and Aldbourne must have been a prehistoric way for it is lined with round barrows. It descends with High Clear Plantation to its right and long views over Four Barrows on Sugar Hill to the left. This track would have been used by John of Gaunt – Shakespeare's 'time honoured Lancaster' – for his journeys between his hunting lodge at Upper Upham and Aldbourne village at the centre of his manor of Aldbourne. It is easy to visualise John of Gaunt, who effectively ruled England during the minority of his nephew Richard II, riding down this track with his entourage, which sometimes would have included his son who became Henry IV and the poet Chaucer, after a day's hunting in Aldbourne Chase.

Old London Road

Prior to the construction of the road along the Kennet Valley in the eighteenth century, the Old London Road from Bristol through Marlborough to London ran east out of Avebury up Green Street and crossed the Ridgeway and Fyfield Down among the sarsen stones. A field on Manton Down is still called London Road Ground, and in 1809 this way was one of Britton's second-class roads. In the Enclosure Award of 1809 it was stipulated that: ' the ancient track called 'Old London Way' to be used at all times as a Public Bridleway and as a private carriage road only for the inhabitants of Overton, Lockeridge, Fyfield, and Clatford respectively'.

Traffic ruts of the Old London Road climbing Overton Down at The Gangway beside Delling Copse (right). The foreground bank survives from the seventeenth century farmstead.

During its heyday early in the eighteenth century this remote way over the Downs would have seen all of London society on its way to take the waters at Bath. This stretch of road which is bleak today let alone in the eighteenth century, was worked by highwaymen. In his story *A Step to Bath* published in 1700 Ned Ward tells of leaving Marlborough by coach and driving across the Downs where the passengers suffered 'confused jolts' from the sarsen stones along the way, and were apprehensive about a warning that 'a party of Light Horse lay hidden, perchance to ease us of our Rino', by which he meant valuables. A comment in the writings of William Stukeley in 1723 suggests that this way over Fyfield Down superceded a way along the Kennet Valley which was later re-opened. Stukeley wrote:

> ... and so they go together above West Kennet to Silbury Hill: this was the post and coach road to Bath, till, for want of reparation, they were forced to find a new one, more northward upon the downs, and farther about, through the town of Abury.

It must have been the hazards and discomforts of the Old London Road which led to the re-opening of the valley route and the building of the many inns along it, including one at West Kennett which offered the renowned Kennett ale described earlier.

Marlborough Turnpike

The north to south Marlborough Turnpike Road from the Swindon area to Marlborough was turnpiked in 1762. Swindon was then of little importance being addressed as 'Swindon, near Highworth'. This road ran along the west edge of Burderop Park where a turnpike cottage survives (164 799) and through Mudgell where it passed west of the old Burderop Racecourse. The road crossed the Ridgeway and climbed Burderop Down passing east of Barbury and then past Four Mile Clump, which is four miles from Marlborough, before reaching Rockley – where there was another turnpike cottage, now gone – on its way to Marlborough. Original milestones survive at Mudgell, Upper Herdswick. Four Mile Clump north of Rockley, at Rockley near the inn site at Old Eagle, and on Marlborough Common.

The intriguing name of Old Eagle arises from the fact that there was an inn here (168 714) called the St. John's Arms after the St. John family

The turnpike road looking north from the 'SWINDON 8, MARLBOROUGH 3' milestone (right) a mile north of Old Eagle. Four Mile Clump is on the horizon.

who owned Rockley in 1795. Their arms incorporated two eagles and it was this inn sign which led to the inn becoming called the Old Eagle by local people. The inn, which became a cottage, was of brick and thatch. It was burned down in December 1947. An old photograph in my possession reveals the Old Eagle Inn to have been such a humble building that it seems likely that it was built as cottages and was adapted to an inn, possibly after becoming a beer house offering refreshment to drovers.

The former Old Eagle Inn near Rockley which was burnt down in 1947. (Drawing by Joe Higham based on a photograph taken by Frances Gay).

More Coach Roads

Sound Bottom (227 711) running west from Ramsbury was for long an alternative to the route (through Hungerford and past Savernake along the line of the present A4) for coach traffic. This way, which was known as 'Ramsbury Narrow Way' descended to Marlborough, and continued to be used until about 1744. According to the *Gentleman's Magazine* for 1752 one determined old Marlborough coachman insisted on continuing to use this way along Sound Bottom – in spite of the wishes of his passengers – on the grounds that it had been followed by both his grandfather and father, who had been coachmen before him. His custom inevitably declined until his four horse team ended up drawing a light passenger fly. It is not known whether he ultimately was persuaded to use the road past Savernake. The Enclosure Agreement for Axford – for which there was no map – describes Sound Bottom as 'London Road', and on it (at 221 715) was a public house called the Black Rabbit, now known as Black Rabbit Barn.

John Britton (1771-1857) was an antiquary and topographer, the son of a small farmer and shopkeeper at Kington St. Michael near Chippenham. When in 1809 he mapped the roads of Wiltshire he classified them as first or second-class roads. Only two first-class roads then crossed the Marlborough Downs. One followed the line of the present A4 west from Marlborough along the valley of the River Kennet to Beckhampton where it forked as now, one branch going to Bath by way of Calne, the other to Devizes. The other first-class road in 1809 was the turnpike road from the Swindon area past Four Mile Clump and Old Eagle to Marlborough. During the mid-nineteenth century Jeremiah Hammond of the Castle and Ball Hotel at Marlborough ran horse-drawn coaches to various destinations, including a service across the Downs along this turnpike road to Swindon. These vehicles were known locally as 'Jerry 'Ammond's buses'.

Britton's mapping of second-class roads is of particular interest since some have now declined into minor trackways and others are mere footpaths. The A4361, which I have taken as the western limit of the Marlborough Downs for this book, was in 1809 a second-class road with a parallel second-class road which is now merely a footpath a little west of it running through the villages of Broad Hinton, Winterbourne Bassett and Berwick Bassett. Another of Britton's second-class roads ran south-east from Winterbourne Bassett past the Totterdowns, but instead of continuing to Marlborough it crossed the Old London Road (at 143 714), and ran south down Clatford Bottom to Clatford and then along Wansdyke and a little north of Bishops Cannings. The Old London Road across Fyfield Down was in 1809 merely a second-class road from Avebury to Marlborough. A further road rated second-class ran south-east from Barbury Castle along Dean Bottom. This has now become a minor trackway. It then turned east and after crossing the Marlborough turnpike (at 168 730) continued along what is now a farm track to Ogbourne St.

Andrew. The road which Cobbett followed from Marlborough to Swindon along the Og Valley was in 1809 only second-class, and two more such roads are shown by Britton running east out of Ogbourne St. George and Ogbourne St. Andrew towards Ramsbury. Both are now mere trackways, the former is today known as Old Chase Road, the other now so unimportant that it has no name. These second-class roads both crossed another old way from Marlborough to Aldbourne which ran as a second-class road past Rabley Wood (as Red Lane) to near Hillwood where (at 239 738) it now becomes a modern road near Lewisham Castle and runs on as Stock Lane to Aldbourne. This route is a much more direct way from Marlborough to Aldbourne than the modern road which passes to the north through Ogbourne St. George.

In 1819 the Og Valley road from Coate past Chiseldon and The Ogbournes to Marlborough was turnpiked, and the old downland way from Swindon to Marlborough past Four Mile Clump went into decline. It was probably about this time or soon after that the Old Eagle Inn near Rockley became cottages although this way over the Downs was followed by 'Jerry 'Ammond's buses' running from Marlborough to Swindon.

Droveways

From Medieval times to the advent of the railways drovers used many of the downland routes across the Marlborough Downs to move their animals the long distance towards London, and the shorter distances to local fairs and markets. The Ridgeway provided an admirable toll-free route eastwards towards London and to the sheep fairs at East Ilsley. In *Villages of the White Horse* Alfred Williams mentions the Shepherd's Rest Inn at Fox Hill as: 'the halting-place of shepherds and drovers in past times' when '80,000 to 100,000 sheep passed this way annually'. Williams also mentioned:

> The Welsh drovers, who brought their herds along Ermin Street, and then passed by the Ridgeway – thereby escaping the charges of tollgates – and wandered leisurely towards their destination, grazing their cattle on the pastures of the hillside.

The avoidance of the tolls which were levied on turnpikes was one of the principal pre-occupations of drovers. Consequently they often used green ways which were parallel to the turnpikes and a short distance from them. Although this toll evasion was their principal attraction to drovers, the green ways offered other advantages. On them the droves were not disrupted by passing coach traffic, and the grass offered grazing for the animals along the route. A good example of a droveway running parallel to a turnpike road is the former green way, now in part a minor tarmacadamed road, which runs south from Chiseldon to Marlborough about a mile west of the turnpike down the Og Valley. This drove road ran past Draycot Foliat and west of Southend to Ogbourne Maizey, where it joined the turnpike road at Bay Bridge. Ponds were of great importance to drovers, especially cattle drovers as cattle require more water than sheep, and a pond lined droveway left the Ridgeway at Glory Ann Pond and ran south-east past Old Totterdown Pond and cottage (138 718) and across Manton Down and Barton Down to Marlborough.

Wansdyke was also used as a well-defined droveway to Tan Hill Fair which was held for hundreds of years beside Wansdyke. From Wansdyke (at 107 646) the Workway Drove ran south-east over the shoulder of Knap Hall into the Vale of Pewsey. Most of the names of the old droveways have now disappeared from the maps, but a few drove names survive on the current Explorer series of Ordnance Survey maps of the Marlborough Downs. These include the Workway Drove just mentioned across Knap Hill, Drove Barn (177 719) situated on Drove Lane west of Ogbourne St. Andrew, Woolmer Drove (195 756) north of Ogbourne St. George, and Copse Lane Drove which climbs Round Hill Downs from Ogbourne St. George towards Aldbourne.

Canals

During the Medieval and post-Medieval periods roads were so bad that many goods were conveyed by boats and barges along rivers, but the Marlborough Downs are so deficient in rivers that water transportation can have had little relevance. Then, in the late eighteenth century, came the canals. No canal crossed the Marlborough Downs, but the Kennet and Avon Canal ran a little to their south along the Vale of Pewsey. It was built in the 1790s and was of importance to the Downs because it provided a cheap means of transporting heavy freight. It was by this canal that during the period from about 1850 to the 1930s sarsen stone was loaded on to barges at Honey Street, after having been carted from the Downs.

The Wilts and Berks Canal passed through Swindon and skirted the north-west edge of the Downs on its way to join the Kennet and Avon Canal near Melksham. There was a wharf at Wroughton, and Richard Jefferies' Coate Water was constructed as a feeder reservoir for this canal, which was abandoned in 1914.

Railways

The railways came to the Marlborough Downs in the 1840s. Following the opening of the Great Western line from London to Bristol through Swindon, the stagecoach traffic along the Great West Road declined rapidly and Marlborough became isolated. Its link with the new railway at Swindon was by a two-horse bus which traversed the Marlborough Downs along the turnpike road past Four Mile Clump. This was an unsatisfactory state of affairs particularly after Marlborough College opened in 1843, but the need for a north-south railway linking Marlborough to Swindon was for long ignored by the Great Western Company. Then in 1881 a line called the Swindon, Marlborough and Andover Railway was opened in spite of opposition from the GWR, linking the Great Western line at Andoversford near Cheltenham with the London and South Western Railway at Andover. This line, which passed through Marlborough and had stations at Chiseldon, Ogbourne St. George and Marlborough, became known as the Midland and South Western Junction Railway. It opened in 1881 amid great rejoicing, for it offered ordinary people of the remote Marlborough Downs the opportunity of cheap and rapid travel to Swindon, and connection to the Great Western Railway system.

The line ran down the valley of the River Og a little west of the main road from Swindon to Marlborough, and then looped east around Marlborough and over the open area between West Woods and Savernake Forest which had once been Savernake Great Park. It was ultimately adopted by the GWR in 1923, and was closed in 1964 after only about eighty years of service.

There is a local story, which I have been unable to confirm, that the last train on this line was derailed because the driver had not been informed that the track had been taken up! Today the line of the railway serves a different transportation use, having in the late 1980s been converted to a cycleway between Marlborough and Chiseldon.

The racehorse trainers of the Marlborough Downs made good use of this railway, as did the Marlborough schoolboys, and padded railway vans were provided from the opening of the line for the safe conveyance of these valuable animals to race-meetings. The existence of the railway must also have influenced the building of the army camps near it in the Og Valley, Chiseldon Camp in the Great War and Ogbourne Camp in the Second World War.

The construction of the railways – first the Great Western in the 1840s and then the Swindon, Marlborough and Andover in the 1870s – was opportune for the residents of the Marlborough Downs in another way, for they provided alternative employment for farm workers at a time when there was severe depression in agriculture. Employment was provided not only in the short term for the construction of the lines, but also in the long term work provided by the Swindon railway works. Alfred Williams moved from poorly paid agricultural work to better paid employment in the railway workshops, and I have heard it said by the elderly son of an agricultural worker who left Snap in about 1900 that he believed that his father was able to move to Swindon and obtain work in the steam-hammer workshop at the railway works – where he knew Alfred Williams – because he had become familiar with steam power on the farm. My informant also told me that his father, who died in about 1921, always regarded his early rural life at Snap as happier than his later urban life at Swindon.

Modern Roads

Early in the twentieth century the roads across the Downs were surfaced with flint extracted from the innumerable 'Flint pits (dis)' of the Ordnance Survey. At that time the flint-surfaced main roads can have been little different from the lesser trackways. These roads were described by Alfred Williams in 1913: 'The material of the road as is usual on the downs is flint. These roads are very hot in summer time; it is stifling to follow the tracks along through the hollows on a brilliant windless day in July or August,' but early in the twentieth century most of the surfaces of the main roads were changed to a bound macadam surface more suitable for the bicycles which became popular after the invention of the pneumatic tyre, and for the motor cars which became available after about 1910.

The 'Old Snape Road' of the 1809 Enclosure Award, running east from Snap to Aldbourne. Along this way the Earl of Essex brought his army of 10,000 foot, 4,000 horse and 15 to 20 field guns after relieving the siege of Gloucester in 1643.

7 Four Upland Villages

It is not proposed to describe the majority of the villages of the Marlborough Downs district. They are adequately described in any number of topographical books, and most are situated at the fringe of the Downs or are in the river valleys and are therefore of little relevance to the downland which is the subject of this book. There are however – or at least there were – four villages which were situated in the high Downs and were so isolated that they have generally escaped the notice of the topographical writers. These are Rockley at the very heart of the Downs, the now-deserted villages of Shaw and Snap, and Upper Upham. Professor Hoskins tells us that 'Hill-top villages are particularly suggestive of high antiquity' and here we have four villages with claims to considerable antiquity which are true upland villages. Rockley stands at an altitude of about 152 metres, Shaw at about 229 metres, Snap at 213 metres, and Upper Upham at about 251 metres.

Rockley

In an article in *Country Life* Geoffrey Grigson described Rockley as offering 'an essence of downland' and as 'essentially part of the historical and prehistorical secrecy of downland.' This is the only village of the four to survive in anything like its early form, although in 1985 its population had reduced to 37 from 103 in 1885. It was listed in Domesday as 'Rochelie', meaning 'rooks' clearing', its name being nothing to do with the sarsen rocks of the area. In late Saxon times Rockley was held by one Alured – later 'Alured de Merlberge' – who succeeded in keeping Rockley which was then assessed at ten hides. There were then seven villagers and twelve borderers.

The Templars, who had a preceptory in nearby Temple Bottom, may have provided a rest-house for pilgrims, and Rockley was known as Temple

Rockley ('Temple-rockley' in the 1591 *Feet of Fines*). From the Knights Templar Rockley passed after their suppression to the Knights Hospitallers, and after the Dissolution Rockley was given by Henry VIII to Sir Edward Bayntun.

Rockley was essentially an agricultural village, and there was an incident here during the agrarian unrest of 1830. In 1855 William Henry Tanner bought the Rockley estate consisting of manor house, seventeen cottages, and 1450 acres of mixed arable and pasture. He built two more cottages, and farmed employing thirty men and two boys. The manor house is comparatively new, being only about two hundred years old. The pond at Rockley, which was probably used by drovers, was very much overgrown but is now restored. Rockley was a noted rendezvous for poachers and an old rustic song called 'In Rockley Firs' was collected by Alfred Williams in *Folk Songs of the Upper Thames*.

Soon after the passing of the 1870 Education Act William Tanner built the tiny school at Rockley, a brick and stone structure with a single room measuring 7.2 by 4 metres. Later a lean-to cloakroom was added. To it came children who used to walk in from the widely dispersed local farms. In 1898 the single mistress wrote of the children in the school log book: 'They still appear lamentably stupid', which could be a reflection on her teaching as much as her pupils' ability! Later, from 1935-47 the sole teacher at Rockley school was Mrs. Frances Gay. The school was finally closed in 1947 by Wiltshire County Council as a result of the low attendance. After it was closed the building was loaned to a Marlborough falconer who piled rocks on the window sills to imitate cliffs in an attempt to persuade his peregrine falcons to breed in captivity. The building still exists, now occupied by a craftsman restoring antiques.

There is evidence for an early church having existed at Rockley, but the present church was built in 1872 and is now disused, having become for a time in the 1980s a well-known local restaurant under the name of 'The Loaves and Fishes' which was I believe a victim of business rates.

Rockley lay a little west of the Swindon to Marlborough coach road and must have surrendered a little of its isolation when that road was turnpiked in 1762. The traffic may even have brought the tiny village a little prosperity for the Old Eagle inn was provided a little south-east of Rockley to cater for travellers on the turnpike and there was also a turnpike gate here. The village has now reverted to its former isolation at the very heart of the Downs.

Mrs Frances J. Gay (1886-1974) who taught at Rockley left an unpublished memoir entitled 'Full Circle' of her time at Rockley. Mrs Gay was a native and resident of Swindon, and Chairman of the Richard Jefferies Society from 1950 to 1971. She was an active campaigner for the preservation of the Jefferies countryside, and is commemorated by a plaque at Coate Water which was dedicated in 1977. Mrs Mary Roberts of Rockley also wrote and published privately *Rockley: A Wiltshire Village* in 1987.

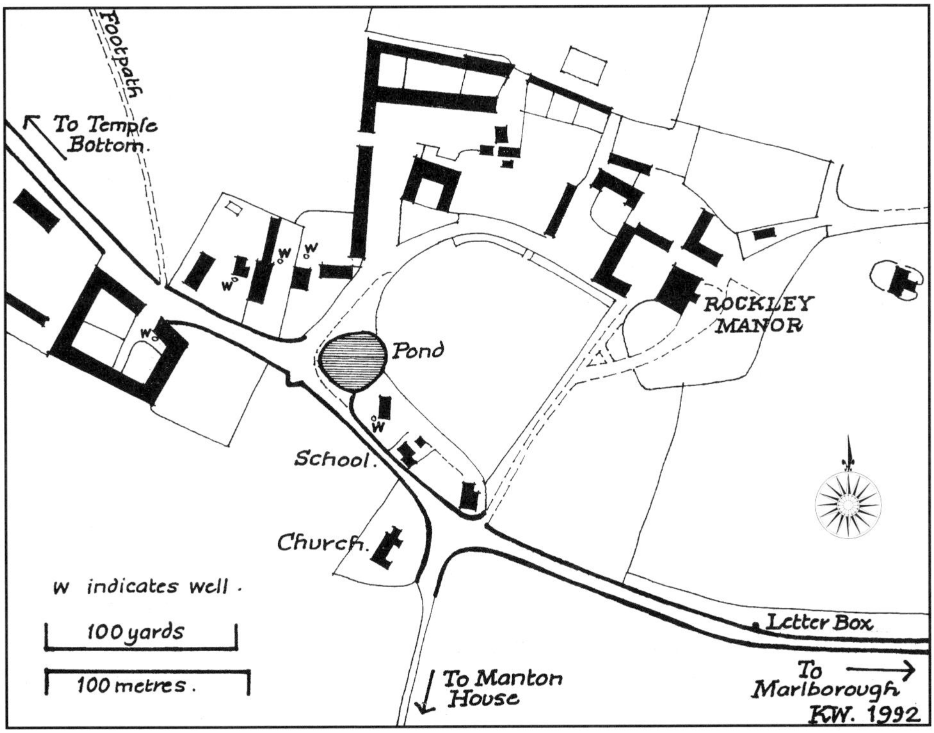

Plan of Rockley village in 1900

Shaw

At Shaw existed a little-known deserted village which is a case of Medieval abandonment. The village existed in 1086 when it was mentioned in Domesday, but little is known about this village for a number of reasons. In the first place access to its remote site (at 138 651 between Alton Priors and Lockeridge towards the south end of the Marlborough Downs) was difficult prior to the opening by agreement with the landowner of the 'permissive' path by which the site is now approached. Anyone wishing to depart from this path in order to examine the site of the village should first obtain the permission of the owner at Shaw Farm, Lockeridge, Marlborough, Wilts. When he excavated the site of Shaw Church in 1929, H.C. Brentnall of Marlborough College remarked in his report on the 'remote field' on which the site was situated. (His excavation reports may be seen in the magazine of *Marlborough College Natural History Society* (No. 78 and in *WAM* 45).

The second complication about the history of Shaw is the fact that a parish boundary runs through its site. This boundary, between Alton Barnes and West Overton, explains references to 'Shaw-in-Alton' and 'Shaw-in-Overton'. A third reason for our want of knowledge is the fact that no records seem to exist. Having searched at the Public Record Office, the British Museum, at Salisbury, and at Winchester, Brentnall was forced to the conclusion that Shaw had no recorded history.

Shaw does however appear in reports defining the limits of jurisdiction of the Forest of Savernake, being situated at the west edge of that forest of which West Woods were formerly part. The word 'shaw' means a small wood, and in Wiltshire was often applied to a narrow strip of woodland. It is derived from the Old English *scaga*, and Shaw went through a number of variants including *Schaga* (1165), *Saghe* (1229), *Schages* (1242), *Shagh* (1279) and *Shawe* (1316). Some of these were applied to Shaw House, now Shaw Farm.

Shaw Church was discovered as a result of Mr. Frederick Stratton of Shaw House telling Mr. Brentnall of a tradition that one of his fields was the site of a former church and, as he believed, the site of a Saxon settlement. Brentnall's excavations established the site and form of the church (at 138 651) which was situated about 100 metres west of Shaw Copse; this was 'Larry's Wood' in 1773 on Andrews and Dury, and on the

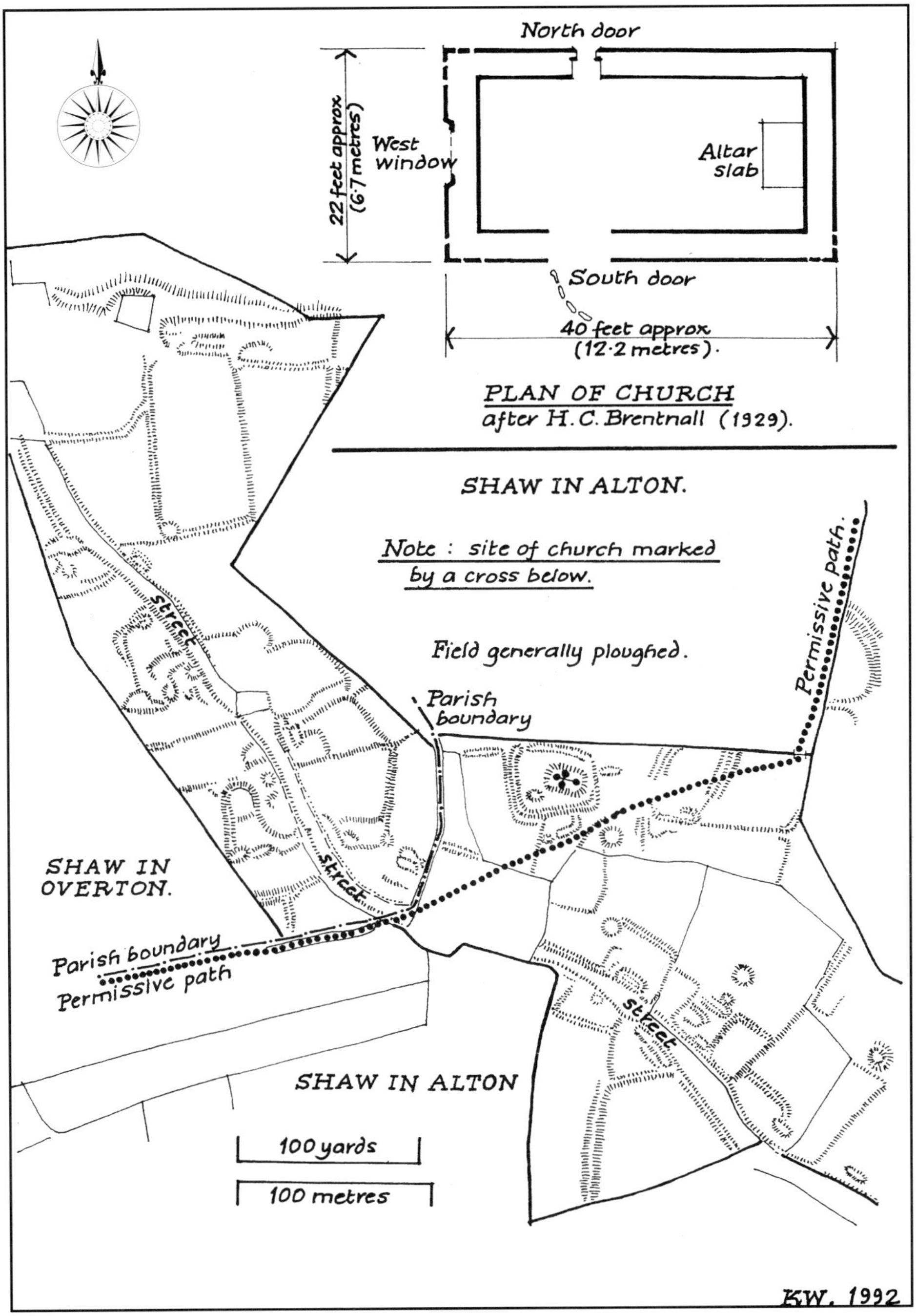

Plan of the earthworks of the deserted Medieval village of Shaw

first Ordnance Survey in about 1820.

The plan produced by Brentnall is of a simple rectangular church with outside dimensions about 12.2 by 6.7 metres, internal about 10.4 by 5.6 metres. The probable seating area of about 7.6 by 3 metres would have accommodated about thirty to thirty-five people seated, although they probably stood, in which case the capacity would be greater. The extremely simple one-cell plan form with no differentiation between sanctuary and nave, together with an apparent lack of buttresses, suggests a very early and possibly Anglo-Saxon date. From the finds Brentnall dated the church as probably early-fourteenth century, but the window which he excavated and photographed – and I wonder where it went – was a simple lancet which looks Early English and therefore probably thirteenth century. This does not necessarily date the church as it could have been an insertion into a church of earlier date.

Tradition asserted that a smithy and many other buildings were associated with Shaw Church, and the extensive earthworks indicate a considerable village with a sunken street. That part of Shaw which lay in Overton parish consists of a hollow-way with some house tofts on either side. It ran north-west towards Wansdyke and also included the site of Shaw Manor. More buildings probably existed in the field between the village and Wansdyke to the immediate north of the church. This is suggested because there are faint signs of earthworks in the plough, because the visible earthworks stop abruptly at the field edge, and because the church had a north door which would have been unlikely if there were no buildings to its north.

The sunken village street was presumably once continuous but was later filled where the 'permissive' path crosses it. Brentnall dug trenches across the churchyard but found no burials. He had neither time nor resources to excavate the village, which remains unexcavated. The date for its desertion is uncertain. The 1377 Poll Tax return was for only three adults – the lowest return in Wiltshire – but this should not be taken to indicate desertion before 1377. The low return may be a reflection of the effects of the Black Death in 1349 and its subsequent outbreaks, and Shaw may later have been re-populated. Shaw was an upland village, remote from water. In this situation it must have been dependant upon sheep-husbandry, and desertion may have occurred in the early-fifteenth century when many upland villages were deserted to make way for more sheep. The local tradition of a church having existed at Shaw may have survived as a result of a nineteenth century endowment of Alton Barnes Church which read: 'On Alton Prior's Down. No. 20a. Churchyard Shaw. Pasture. 1 rood, 15 poles'.

During his investigations into Wansdyke, Sir Richard Colt Hoare seems to have had no inkling of the former existence of Shaw village, although in his 'Summer Campaign, 1806' notes to his collaborator William Cunnington he wrote: 'Go to Shaw farm, built upon the dyke and examine some meadows to the west of the house, which are full of irregularities'. This sounds like a reference to the village site, but Shaw was definitely to the east of Shaw Farm, not to the 'west'. Cunnington may have dug at Shaw because he wrote: 'being in sight of the house we could dig in only two places'.

The site of Shaw village is a capping of clay-with-flints over underlying chalk. This explains the many trees which obscure the aerial photographs of the site held by the archaeological section of Wiltshire Library and Museum Service at Trowbridge. If Shaw was indeed an Anglo-Saxon village as its mention in Domesday suggests, its situation beside Wansdyke is of interest. We have seen that Wansdyke may have been built as a frontier between the West Saxons of Wessex and the Upper Thames Saxons to the north, and that battles were fought at Adam's Grave less than two miles south-west of Shaw. In those troubled times Shaw may have been a frontier village, perhaps providing some of the manpower used both to construct and defend Wansdyke against incursions from the north.

Snap

The deserted village of Snap in Aldbourne Chase was situated between the villages of Woodsend and Upper Upham, about three miles west of Aldbourne (at 223 765). It is of particular interest due to the fact that it is an example which is in general unusual and in Wiltshire unique of a village finally deserted and destroyed in the early twentieth century as a result of agricultural depression of the late-nineteenth century. In the late nineteenth century Snap was a tiny linear village of about seven cottages with Snap Farm at its west end. It never had a church or chapel, relying for these on Woodsend up the hill, but there was once a dame school in

EAST END OF SNAP LOOKING EAST
reconstructed from a photograph in the 'Daily Mirror' on 12th July 1913.

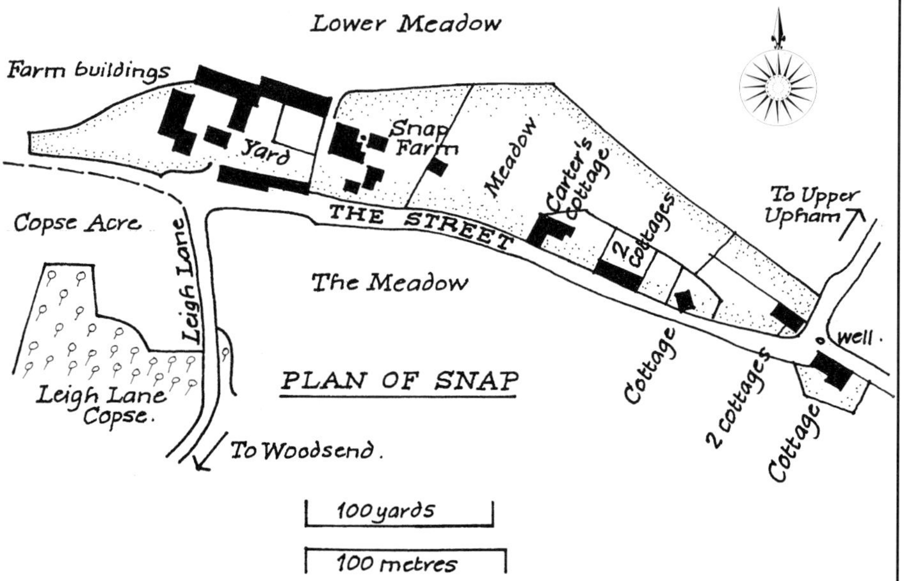

KW. 1992

one of the cottages. The village was of early origin having been recorded as *Snape* in 1268 and gone through later variations such as *Snappe* in 1332 and *Snape* and *Snapp* in the nineteenth century. The name is believed to be derived from *snaep* meaning boggy ground, the village being near the bottom of a little coombe; the name could be of Norse origin.

Nineteen adults paid Poll Tax at Snap in 1377 but there is little recorded history because the place was so tiny and unimportant. Interest in Snap began with the circumstances of its abandonment. The 1841 census reveals that there were then forty-seven persons at Snap, all dependant upon the sheep and corn husbandry of the local farm. When cheap corn began to pour into England from America in the 1870s the writing was on the wall for Snap and agricultural depression set in.

The villagers struggled on until the end of the century. In 1851 there were 41 residents, in 1861 there were 53, in 1871 only 47, and by 1881 the population was significantly down to 34. From this date numbers declined rapidly as the young men drifted away in search of work. The terminal blow for the village came in 1905 after the departure of most of the villagers when Mr. Henry Wilson, a butcher from Ramsbury, bought Snap and the surrounding farms to graze his stock. Soon there were only four old people at Snap, the Smiths and the Fishers, all in their eighties. Both the Smiths and James Fisher died, leaving Rachel Fisher alone in the deserted village. She was ultimately persuaded to move into Aldbourne where she died.

Henry Wilson has been unfairly blamed for the depopulation of Snap in several emotive articles in the press, including a grossly inaccurate one in the *Daily Mirror* on 12 July 1913. He had acquired a village which was already effectively abandoned, but he was blamed for depriving the villagers of their homes. Mr. Wilson's sons, after he had died in 1911, sued Mr. Lambert the local M.P. for defaming the character of their father, and periodically more inaccurate articles have appeared on the 'butcher of Ramsbury' theme.

Today nearly all signs of the cottages at Snap have gone, although piles of sarsen rubble may be seen occupying their positions in winter when the site is not overgrown. To those who are aware that a village existed here for hundreds of years and has now disappeared practically without trace the site has an air of melancholy. Access is by the byway down the former village street, but the sites of the cottages are private land which should not be entered as deep wells may have been boarded over, and the boards may have rotted.

When I wrote my book on Snap, I concluded it with a quotation from Masefield's 'August 1914' which so aptly sums up the melancholy feelings evoked by the deserted site that I quote it again here:

> 'These houses, this valley spread below me here,
> The rooks, the tilted stacks, the beasts in pen,
> Have been the heartfelt things, past-speaking dear
> To unknown generations of dead men.....
>
> Surely above these fields a spirit broods
> A sense of many watchers muttering near
> Of the lone downland with the forlorn woods
> Loved to the death, inestimably dear.'

In 1991 a class of nine-year-old children at Toothill School in Swindon enthusiastically undertook a project on Snap, and as a result in August 1991 a stone commemorating its former villagers was erected at Snap, paid for by subscriptions raised by their teacher Mr. Brian Gardner.

Upper Upham

The deserted Medieval village of Upper Upham was situated west of Upham Manor House (at 225 774). This area is known to have been occupied since very early times and Professor Fowler has suggested Upper Upham as one of the few downland villages to have 'a continuous history of settlement since Romano-British times'. Coins of most periods have been found in the area and Upham was recorded as *Uphammere* in 955; in the 1377 Poll Tax returns forty adults were listed at Upper Upham. This village was part of Aldbourne Manor and as such was acquired by John of Gaunt, Duke of Lancaster, in the mid-fourteenth century. As part of the Duchy of Lancaster estates Upper Upham went to the Crown in 1399 when John of Gaunt died. That same year his son Henry, who would certainly have known Upham, under great provocation from the king usurped the throne of Richard II and became king as Henry IV.

Upham Manor had been John of Gaunt's hunting lodge when he hunted Aldbourne Chase, and Upham village may have been depopulated to make way for a deer park to the west of the manor house. Around this area there is a distinct linear earthwork which I believe could be the remains of a park-pale bank and ditch. This theory gains some credence from the fact that a *Calendar Patent Roll* entry in 1307 refers to a deer park and right of free warren at Aldbourne, owned by Henry de Lacy, Earl of Lincoln (c1249-1311), who was a close friend of Edward I. No signs of a deer park are evident today at or near Aldbourne village, but deer parks were often created on poor land at an extremity of the parish where they interfered least with the life of the village. Upper Upham qualifies on both counts, being at the western edge of Aldbourne parish on ground which was very poor prior to the introduction of artificial fertilizers in the nineteenth century. There is also the fact that John of Gaunt used Upham as a hunting lodge, having acquired it in 1365 less than sixty years after the above 1307 reference to a deer park. As the son of Edward III, John of Gaunt was an extremely powerful man who as an enthusiastic hunter created deer parks at many of his estates. He was quite capable of dispossessing a few Upham villagers of their homes in order to create or enlarge his deer park. There are frequent references to a park which existed at Snap, and Snap is situated merely half a mile south of Upper Upham.

At the Dissolution of the monasteries in 1539 Upper Upham was in the hands of the Abbess of Lacock who had in 1527 leased it to John Goddard, 'woolman', for grazing. Henry VIII – no doubt for a 'consideration' – transferred ownership of Upham to John Goddard and it was this acquisition which consolidated the fortunes of the Goddards, the great landowning family of north-east Wiltshire.

The Goddards built an Elizabethan manor house at Upper Upham, probably on the site of John of Gaunt's hunting lodge, although the lodge may have occupied another site. Upham always experienced difficulty over water supply due to its elevated position, and it is said that when John of Gaunt was here he used to go to Aldbourne for his baths. As late as the nineteenth century Richard Jefferies recorded that Upper Upham, which he knew well, was dependant upon the donkey well at Snap for its water.

The house is built of stone and flint with stone slated roof. It boasts an elaborate south-east front with on its porch the date 1599, the initials

Elizabethan manor house at Upper Upham;
Above: after reconstruction and extension in about 1910;
Below: before reconstruction, from a postcard

of Thomas Goddard, and those of his son Richard and wife Elizabeth who completed the house in 1599. The plainer north-west front is embellsihed with a fine coat of arms. The house became derelict in the nineteenth century, and when Jefferies knew it the house was occupied by a labourer with whom he was friendly. In about 1910 it was purchased by Miss Hanham (1872-1939) who married Sir James Curry in 1913, and it was at this time that they sensitively extended the house, retaining its Elizabethan style. The name of Lutyens has been associated with the extensions, but according to Pevsner and the *Victoria County History* the architect of the large wing added to the west was Biddulph Pinchard. Today the manor house is in shared occupancy, and some new development has taken place at Upper Upham. In the 1960s a red-brick crescent of large semi-detached houses was built west of the manor house and south of the Medieval village site and a red brick farmhouse has been built in a very prominent position south of the big house.

Proof of the existence of these four upland villages in the fourteenth century, together with an indication of the comparable wealth of their residents, is contained in the returns resulting from Parliament's grant of taxes to Edward III in 1332. At *Snappe* taxes totalling 6s.10d. (34p) were levied against six payers, at Upham nine taxpayers paid a total of 28s.10d. (£1.44p) and a total of 6s.5d. (32p) was paid by six taxpayers at *Shawe*. At *Roucle* (Rockley) 71s.3d. (£3.56p) was paid by twelve taxpayers, of which the Master of the Knights of the Hospital paid 44s.6d. (£2.22p).

The former existence of another now lost Medieval upland village at Barbury is indicated by the fact that five taxpayers paid 9s.4d. (47p) at *Berebury*, which is almost half as much again as was levied at Snap. The site of the village at Barbury was probably between Barbury Castle Farm and the hillfort to its north, within the little coombe where earthworks exist (152 758).

RICHARD JEFFERIES
1848-1887
'From the blue hill lines, from the dark copses on the ridges, the shadows in the combes... there comes from these an influence which forces the heart to lift itself in earnest and purest desire.'

ALFRED WILLIAMS 1877-1930
'The slopes of the downs, if they have general forms, are continually changing and interchanging in localities, assuming new and strange shapes, charming and surprising wiuth their grace and exquisiteness... for ever reflecting the mood of the heavens, and sympathetic to the heart and feelings of men.'

EDWARD THOMAS
1878-1917
This is pure downland; the breasted hills curving as if under the influence of a great melody. It is a beautiful, a quiet, an unrenowned and a most visibly ancient land.

8 The Literary and Artistic Scene

In recent years great interest has been shown in places associated with writers and many people derive pleasure from making literary pilgrimages to such places. It was inevitable that the multitude of aesthetic, historical and archaeological attractions which are concentrated into the comparatively small area of the Marlborough Downs should have attracted writers of many periods. This chapter is not concerned with the purely topographical or archaeological writers such as Stukeley, Colt Hoare, Timperley, Massingham and Grinsell. Its subjects are the men of wider literary horizons who made their mark on the national literary scene but were also associated with this area, writers and poets such as Richard Jefferies, Alfred Williams, Edward Thomas and Charles Sorley.

Richard Jefferies

The writer most closely associated with the Marlborough Downs is Richard Jefferies (1848-87), a writer of considerable standing who is regarded as a worthy successor to White of Selborne and has been described as 'the prose poet of the English countryside'. Jefferies was native to this area, being born the son of a small farmer at Coate Farm near the north edge of the Marlborough Downs. He wrote almost exclusively in prose, first as a local newspaper reporter and then as a local historian. Having failed as a novelist, for which his solitary rural and unsocial life had ill-equipped him, he became known as a result of some perceptive letters on rural matters which were printed in *The Times* in 1872. He now discovered his métier in essays and books on rural subjects based on the considerable knowledge which he had acquired wandering his native countryside which included the Marlborough Downs.

In 1877 at the age of twenty-nine Jefferies left Wiltshire to be nearer the literary opportunities available in London, but his nature writings continued to be based on his experiences in Wiltshire, and many of his books contain references to the Marlborough Downs. These books included *The Gamekeeper at Home* (1878), *The Amateur Poacher* (1879), *Wildlife in a Southern County* (1879), *Hodge and His Masters* (1880), *Round About a Great Estate* (1880) and *The Story of My Heart* (1883). *Wildlife in a Southern County* contains a description of the Ridgeway:

> A broad green track runs for many a long, long mile across the downs, now following the ridges, now winding past at the foot of a grassy slope, then stretching away through cornfield and fallow. It is distinct from the wagon-tracks which cross it here and there, for these are local only, and, if traced up, land the wayfarer presently in a maze of fields, or end abruptly in the rickyard of a lone farmhouse. It is distinct from the hard roads of modern construction which also at wide intervals cross its course, dusty and glaringly white in the sunshine. It is not a farm track – you may walk for twenty miles along it over the hills; neither is it the king's highway.

Alfred Williams

Another native writer inevitably associated with the Downs is Alfred Williams (1877-1930), a working man who was for long employed in the steam-hammer shop at Swindon railway works. Williams, who wrote both poetry and prose, contrived to educate himself to a high standard and learn several languages in his spare time. He was born and died at South Marston, east of Swindon and a little north of the Marlborough Downs which he knew, loved, and described as 'sweetly and chastely beautiful, and unsurpassed in interest' (*Villages of the White Horse*: 1913). Alfred Williams spent much of his time collecting folk-songs, and like Jefferies wrote much local history, some of it about the Downs where his favourite resort was Barbury Castle.

Both Jefferies and Williams are commemorated by a standing sarsen stone which was erected east of Barbury on Burderop Down (at 158 763) in December 1939. It bears two plaques with inscriptions from both Jefferies and Williams which read:

'It is Eternity now, I am in the midst of it,
It is about me in the sunshine.'

from Chapter 3 of *The Story of My Heart*, and:

'Still to find and still to follow,
Joy in every field and hollow
Company in solitude.'

from *Songs in Wiltshire* by Alfred Williams. These two writers are also commemorated by a plaque fixed to the Ordnance Survey trigonometrical point on Liddington Hill. Of Alfred Williams no less a person than the poet laureate Robert Bridges wrote; 'His achievement is an abiding spiritual example to the workmen of his country.'

Edward Thomas

A writer who was not a Wiltshireman but virtually became one by 'adoption' was Edward Thomas (1878-1917). He developed his strong affinity with Wiltshire during boyhood holidays spent with his paternal grandmother in the railway village at Swindon where he became in his own words 'a Wiltshire boy in accent'. Thomas was born in London of Welsh parents and went to Lincoln College at Oxford where he obtained a degree in history. He then decided to live by writing, despite parental opposition. Edward Thomas was an admirer of Richard Jefferies and in 1907 was commissioned to write a biography of him. The research for this book extended his already considerable knowledge of north-east Wiltshire, and the first chapter of *Richard Jefferies: His Life and Work* (1909) provides probably the best introduction to the Marlborough Downs produced to date. Many of the prose works of Edward Thomas refer to the Marlborough Downs, for example his speculation about the origin of the place-name Glory Ann in his introduction to Isaac Taylor's *Words and Places* (1911).

Thomas is now very highly regarded as a poet. In the last three years of his life, when the Great War caused his 'hack work' to dry up, he amused himself by writing the poetry on which his considerable reputation now rests, and found himself 'engrossed as I never was in prose'. He was killed at Arras on Easter Monday, 1917, and is commemorated by a sarsen stone from the Marlborough Downs which was set up in 1937 on the Shoulder of Mutton Hill near Steep in Hampshire where he lived. (This stone was selected by another poet, Andrew Young (1885-1971), a Scotsman who loved English downland and wrote a poem entitled 'Wiltshire Downs' which is included in the *Oxford Book of Twentieth Century English Verse*).

Charles Sorley

Charles Hamilton Sorley (1895-1915) was, like Edward Thomas, a victim in the Great War. His early death before his potential was more than hinted at was a sad loss to literature. His letters and poems have been collected. In 1908 Sorley went to Marlborough College which he attended until 1913. Marlborough he loved, and the Downs in wind, mist and rain. He left Marlborough with great regret. At the outbreak of war in 1914 he was in Germany at the University of Jena as a student of philosophy. He deplored the war between two countries he loved. With some difficulty he succeeded in crossing into Belgium, and it is ironic that, had he failed to escape, he would have been interned for the duration and escaped the sniper's bullet which terminated his life at the age of twenty.

Sorley's most-anthologised poem is 'The Song of the Ungirt Runners' in which he celebrates cross-country runs in the Marlborough Downs 'Through the great wide air.... Neath the big bare sky....Through the broad bright land'. Even more relevant to my subject is the long poem entitled 'Marlborough' written 1 March 1914, from which the following is extracted:

> 'I who have walked along her downs in dreams,
> And known her tenderness and felt her might,
> And sometimes by her meadows and her streams
> Have drunk deep-storied secrets of delight,
>
> Have had my moments there, when I have been
> Unwittingly aware of something more,
> Some beautiful aspect that I had seen
> With mute unspeculative eyes before;

Have had my times, when, though the earth did wear
Her self-same trees and grasses,I could see
The revelation that is always there,
But somehow is not always clear to me.'

Other poems by Sorley about places in the Marlborough Downs include 'Barbury Camp' (written 1913) and 'Richard Jefferies (Liddington Castle)' (1913).

One of Sorley's favourite places on the Downs was Four Mile Clump, the vantage point on the Swindon turnpike four miles from Marlborough, which he referred to in another poem as 'Four Miler's Heights'. As he was killed on the Western Front aged only twenty, Sorley's association with the Marlborough Downs was as a schoolboy at Marlborough College. He was the son of Professor Sorley at Cambridge, and when at the start of term he returned to Marlborough from Cambridge he would leave the train in the Berkshire Downs and walk past East Ilsley along the Ridgeway where, he recorded in a letter, he 'turned at right angles on to the top of that other ridge that runs east of the road from Swindon to Marlborough, and separates Wilts and Berks [sic], and on its back I threaded my way back to Marlborough.' Sorley was mistaken about the position of the Wilts-Berks boundary, but it seems that from Liddington Castle he followed the escarpment which runs southwards and west of Upper Upham and Snap and east of Ogbourne St. George past Rabley Wood to Marlborough.

Other Writers

Jefferies, Williams, Thomas and Sorley are the writers most particularly associated with the Marlborough Downs, but a number of other literary men are more loosely connected with the area.

Thomas Hardy (1840-1928) was of course very much a Dorset writer, but he has a connection with the Marlborough Downs which appear as 'Marlbury Downs' on the map which he drew to be incorporated in his Wessex novels. These Downs provided the location for 'What the Shepherd Saw' which was centred upon the Devil's Den in Clatford Bottom a little north of the A4. This appears in Hardy's tale as 'The Devil's Door' with the shepherd boy's hut at 'Lambing Corner', a real or imaginary place which I have failed to identify.

Prior to the construction of the road along the Kennet Valley it has been noted that the London Road to Bristol crossed Fyfield Down from Marlborough to Avebury. During the seventeenth and early-eighteenth centuries most of London society would have crossed the Marlborough Downs by this road on their way to take the waters at Bath, but few left any account of their journey since at that time wild countryside was regarded with awe and horror. That industrious diarist Samuel Pepys (1633-1703) left us a short account of his journey. On Monday 15 June 1668, after being at Bath and Bristol, Pepys visited Avebury and Silbury Hill on his way back to London, and wrote in his diary:

> ...it was prodigious to see how full the downs are of great stones, and all along the valleys stones of considerable bigness most of them growing certainly out of the ground so thick as to cover the ground.

The inclusion by Charles Dickens (1812-1870) of 'The Ghost of Pit Pond' in *Household Words* (1867) might be taken as an indication that Dickens was familiar with the Marlborough Downs. The story tells how Farmer Reeves of Huish Farm at the south edge of the Downs hanged himself in one of his barns and haunted Pit Pond at Huish after being rejected by a girl who was brought to his farm to recover after a riding accident on the Downs. An extract from the story has already been told in connection with Martinsell Hill, but the entire story had been printed by Dudley Costello in the *Piccadilly Annual* for 1848 and Dickens may have borrowed the story from there.

The poet W.H. Davies (1871-1940) who in 1907 published with the encouragement of Edward Thomas *The Autobiography of a Super Tramp*, walked the road from Calne to Marlborough when writing *A Poet's Pilgrimage*. He lets fall that he 'had travelled this road from Calne to Marlborough in my real tramp's days', but by the time he was writing *A Poet's Pilgrimage* he had achieved respectability and real standing as a poet of, for example, 'What is this life if, full of care. We have no time to stand and stare?'. On his pilgrimage Davies was preoccupied with the beggars and tramps he met along the way, and took scant notice of the scenery of the Marlborough Downs. He does however mention a stop at the Waggon and Horses at Beckhampton; Davies never passed a public house without entering lest he should offend the landlord by withholding his custom! He had a wooden leg as a result of an injury sustained when jumping a train in America, and I seldom pass the Waggon and Horses without imagining a suitably refreshed Davies stumping out of the door to resume his pilgrimage.

In 1821 William Cobbett (1763-1835) came to this area on his *Rural Rides*. His account of the ride from Marlborough to Swindon has already been quoted in Chapter 5.

The poet, designer, craftsman and socialist William Morris (1834-1896) loved the Marlborough Downs, having developed an interest in archaeology and history when he was at Marlborough College. Games were not compulsory at Marlborough and Morris spent his games half-days exploring the antiquities of the area. His description in a letter of a water meadow is quoted in Chapter 4.

More recently the former Poet Laureate Sir John Betjeman (1906-84) attended Marlborough College 1920-1925, and wrote of his experiences there in prose and poetry. References to places such as Manton Lane and Hackpen Hill occur in his verse autobiography *Summoned by Bells*, and he wrote of the haunting atmosphere of Avebury 'on a still moonlit night when it seems to be peopled with ghosts, and the old church and cottages of the village seem quite new and insignificant.' This is reminiscent of the Wiltshire writer Edith Olivier's belief that in October 1916 she was transposed back in time at Avebury and witnessed an eighteenth century fair among the stones.

Geoffrey Grigson (1905-1985), poet, reviewer, broadcaster and writer, was the author of *The Shell Country Alphabet* (1966), a useful work of reference which reveals his encyclopaedic knowledge of the countryside. He lived for the latter half of his life at Broad Town under the western escarpment of the Marlborough Downs. Grigson wrote many essays and books concerned with aspects of the Downs, and provided the text for the beautifully produced little Thames and Hudson picture book entitled *The Wiltshire Book* (1957). Let into the wall of his house – Broad Town Farmhouse – are tablets inscribed with some of his poems concerned with gardening. Geoffrey Grigson was also an authority on wild flowers, and wrote *The Englishman's Flora* (1955) and *Dictionary of English Plant Names* (1974).

A final admittedly tenuous literary connection with the Marlborough Downs is the fact that in the late 1930s some of the first active efforts to preserve the Avebury landscape by preventing a proposed housing development at Waden Hill and by helping The National Trust to acquire the Avebury monument were in part financed from the trust fund set up from the royalties from Lawrence of Arabia's (1888-1935) *Seven Pillars of Wisdom*. This trust was administered by Lawrence's younger brother A.W. Lawrence (1900-1991) who to the end of his life continued to support the vital land acquisitions by The National Trust in the Avebury area.

Artists

Paul Nash (1889-1946), who painted surreal and imaginative landscapes, knew Edward Thomas with whom he served in the Artists' Rifles before becoming an official war artist in 1917, in which capacity he also served in the Second World War. In 1933 he suffered a severe attack of bronchitis, and whilst recuperating at Marlborough discovered the megaliths at Avebury which inspired a series of paintings, including 'Landscape of the Megaliths'. In 'Picture History' Paul Nash left a description in writing of Avebury prior to the Keiller reconstruction:

> The preoccupation of the stones has always been a separate pursuit and interest aside from that of object personages. My interest began with the discovery of the Avebury megaliths when I was staying at Marlborough in the Summer of 1933. The great stones were then in their wild state, so to speak. Some were half covered by the grass, others stood up in the cornfields were entangled and overgrown in the copses, some were buried under the turf. But they were always wonderful and disquieting, and, as I saw them then, I shall always remember them...Their colouring and pattern, their patina of golden lichen, all enhanced their strange forms and mystical significance. Thereafter, I hunted stones, by the seashore, on the downs, in the furrows. In most instances, the pictures coming out of this preoccupation were concerned with stones seen solely as objects in relation to landscape as in the 'Landscape of the Megaliths' series, or as stone objects related to other objects, or groups of objects.

At this time Nash wrote to his wife: 'If anything will preserve my interest in landscape from a painter's point of view it will be this country'.

The painter John Piper (1903-1992) knew the Wiltshire Downs as a boy when he became a member of the Wiltshire Archaeological Society. From 1939-1950 he was a close friend of Geoffrey Grigson. His great interest was in architecture and as editor of the series he collaborated with J.H. Cheetham – an architect – in writing the third edition of *The Shell Guide to Wiltshire* (1968). He loved Avebury Stone Circle and once commented upon its 'inconsequent domesticity'. In 1981 Piper designed a stained glass window for Devizes Museum and in it incorporated archaeological elements from the Marlborough Downs including the stones of West Kennett Avenue, the Devil's Den dolmen, and several round barrows.

Composers

Although the Marlborough Downs seem to have few associations with music two of England's finest twentieth century pastoral composers are connected with the district. Ralph Vaughan Williams (1872-1958) was born at Down Ampney on the Wiltshire-Gloucestershire border, and was living at Sheepshanks Cottage at Marlborough in July 1911 when he wrote part of his once very popular ballad opera 'Hugh the Drover', and during the summer of 1924 he composed 'Flos Campi' at a house called Martinscote in Oare village. His follower Gerald Finzi (1901-1956), who has an ever-growing reputation, intermittently lived at Beech Knoll, Aldbourne. During a long stay from 1933 to 1939 he wrote 'Dies Natalis' – his setting of Traherne – 'Two Milton Sonnets', and 'Earth and Air and Rain', the latter being no doubt influenced by the landscape and climate of the Marlborough Downs, where he particularly loved Suygar Hill.

Early in this century Alfred Williams devoted much of his time to collecting folk songs in this area and the Vale of White Horse. These were published as *Songs in Wiltshire* (1909) and *Folk Songs of Upper Thames* (1923).

The Hartigan Cemetery situated in the Downs near The Ogbournes, sometimes known as 'The Horseman's Grave'

9 The Recent Past
(since about 1850)

Recent developments have to date fortunately left the Marlborough Downs comparatively unspoiled. The area has been included in the North Wessex Downs Area of Outstanding Natural Beauty, and The National Trust is busily acquiring land around Avebury in order to preserve it for the nation. The M4 motorway has been carved across the Downs a little south of Swindon but has discreetly skirted the north edge of the Marlborough Downs. During two World Wars the military came to this area but – unlike on Salisbury Plain – in due course departed. In the Great War an army camp was built at Chiseldon and Snap was used as a target for artillery practice, and during the Second World War another camp was built at Ogbourne St. George, but both camps have now been removed. It seems that the first Chiseldon Camp must have been cleared away after the First World War because in 1919 Alfred Williams built his house 'Ranikhet', at South Marston, out of 'very good timber from Chiseldon Camp' (letter to Lord Fitzmaurice). During the Second World War the many American soldiers at Ogbourne Camp are said to have included the world heavyweight boxing champion Joe Louis. Pillboxes were built during the Second World War in strategic positions with a view to resisting impending invasion. A line of pillboxes was constructed through the site of the former Savernake Great Park west of Savernake Forest, presumably to defend the railway line which formerly crossed this area. It is a strange coincidence that this twentieth century line of defence against an invasion by the Germans very nearly coincided with the defensive line of Wansdyke which may have been built in the sixth century by the Britons to resist the advance of the Saxons, a Germanic people who originated in the region of the Lower Elbe.

Modern Farming

During the 1870s Britain suffered severe agricultural depression as cheap wheat poured into the country from the newly-opened grain-growing plains of the American west. This was followed by cheap meat from the Argentine and New Zealand made possible by following the introduction of the first refrigerated ship in 1869. The effects of the depression are exemplified in the Marlborough Downs by the story of Snap. The resultant unemployment among agricultural workers was alleviated in this area by employment offered by the railway companies in constructing the railway lines and the continuing employment provided by the vast Great Western Railway factory which had been opened at Swindon.

Farming today in these Downs consists of a mixture of arable and grazing. The high downs which were formerly reserved as sheepwalks are now often grazed by cattle, referred to by Richard Jefferies as 'young things', and the tractor-drawn plough creeps ever higher up the Downs and sometimes goes literally over the top. Ploughing of the Downs was facilitated first by the introduction of the steam plough which was invented at Baydon. In 1855 Mr. J.A. Williams of Baydon patented improvements in steam machinery for driving ploughs. One of his inventions was portable steam engines driving winding drums. John Fowler (1826-1880) – another Wiltshireman from Melksham – improved on the idea. He had been mole-ploughing drains, and in 1852 had replaced his horses with a steam engine. He saw the potential of Williams's drum system and in January 1856 patented the idea for a stationary steam engine driving a double capstan and his first steam plough went to work on 10 April 1856.

In spite of the local invention of the steam plough, ox-ploughing continued to be practised in this area well into the twentieth century. In 1883 Jefferies wrote of 'four oxen drawing the ancient wheeled plough', and as late as 1910 a team of oxen from Aldbourne Warren Farm were exhibited in London. Oxen were said to have several advantages over horses for ploughing. They were hardier, pulled steadier, ate rougher food and ate it more rapidly, and after they had worked about ten years they – again in the words of Richard Jefferies – made 'prime meat in due time'. Jefferies also pointed out that 'you cannot fatten and dine on a steam plough'. Oxen were also used as draught animals to pull carts and rollers, but their disadvantage was said to be that they had an infallible sense of time and refused to work after three o'clock!

Today ox, horse and steam ploughing are long obsolete. The First World War encouraged the development of the internal combustion engine and ploughing is now done by a tractor driver in a weatherproof and sometimes air-conditioned cab with entertainment laid on through headphones. One cannot but applaud such progress from the hard slog of former times, for the old multi-week harvest is now achieved in a few days as a result of mechanised petrol-driven tractors drawing huge multi-shared ploughs. Romantics may long nostalgically for the old days depicted in early photographs of the horse-drawn plough and waggon, the harvesters in their smocks in fields of stooked corn and the women field workers assisting in their poke-bonnets, but these were days of utter drudgery, degradation and poverty for the agricultural workers. They may have been happy because they knew no better, but their existence was very precarious with the workhouse always looming.

The farming of rabbits in warrens up to the early-nineteenth century has already been described. Warrening continued into the twentieth century on Fyfield Down where the sarsen stones were such a hindrance to agriculture, but in 1910 the rabbits were finally got rid of. The rabbits used to be gutted in the shed beside Delling Cottage (135 712) before being sent off by the cartload to game dealers in London. This cottage, in its extremely remote situation, was probably built as the warrener's lodge.

A recent feature of arable farming has been the practice, driven by economic considerations, of reducing the input of weedkillers. This has caused corn-fields to revert to their appearance of many years ago with red poppies sprinkling the crops and beautifying the other-wise bland appearance of a corn crop extending over the vast areas of modern fields. It may not be good farming, but from the aesthetic point of view it is very pleasing, and the reduced use of fertilizers and weedkillers has brought another noticeable and tangible benefit in the decrease in plastic bags discarded by farm workers and littering the countryside.

Far less pleasing than poppies in the corn, in my estimation, is the annual onset in April of vast fields of oil-seed rape which has been extensively grown since about 1980. Every year 'Englands green and pleasant land' is now subjected to an eruption of crude yellow flowers in solid mass. I particularly dislike the intrusiveness of rape which is so

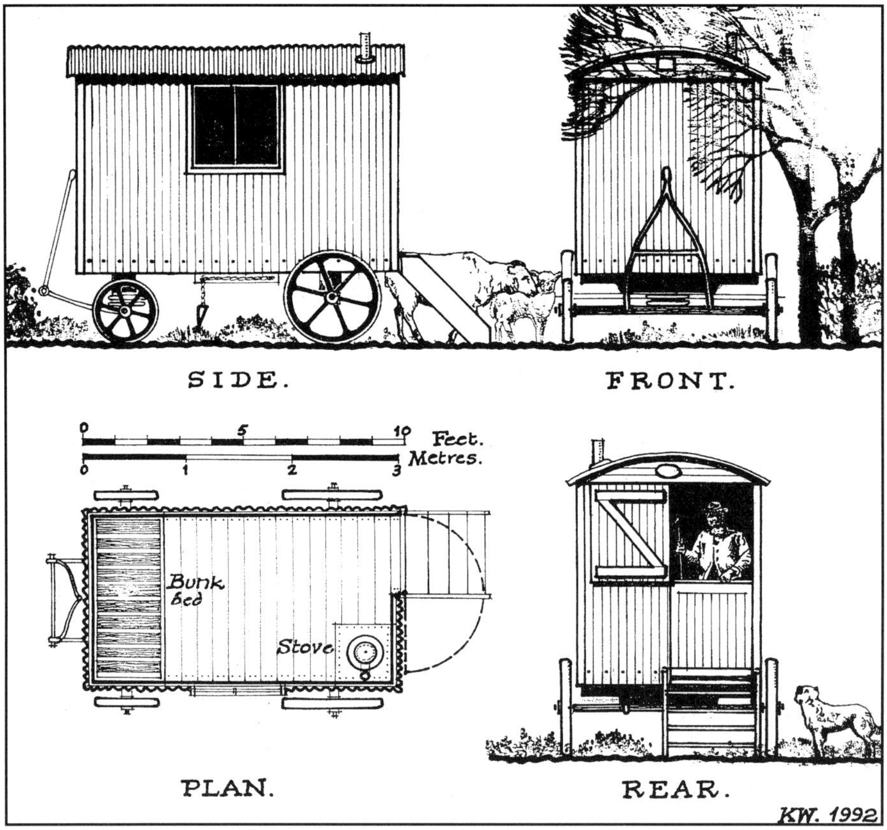

Above: Typical shepherd's hut (drawn by the author)

Right: Derelict shepherd's hut south of Liddington Hill

disruptive of the subtlety of downland landscape, particularly when account is taken of its objectionable smell and rumours of possible side effects.

Fortunately, since about 1988, the popularity of rape has to some extent waned in favour of a visually far more acceptable crop. Linseed – also known as flax – was formerly widely grown but for many years went out of favour. In 1945 H.J. Massingham wrote of a revival in flax growing (in *The Wisdom of the Fields*) and noted that the Avebury area was particularly well-suited for this crop, but flax went completely out of fashion and was rarely grown until recently.

The flax which is now grown is not the form which was retted for linen, but a variety rich in linseed which is used for linseed oil and cattle feed. Farmers generally refer to it as linseed rather than as flax. In July the flax fields turn a beautiful dusty blue as the plants come into flower and attract the attention of passers-by who often enquire: 'What crop is that?'. After noon, and when the sun goes in, the flax flowers tend to close. This crop is particularly difficult to harvest as its tough stems tangle in the machinery. John Moore described a flax field in *The Blue Field* (1948) as 'this astonishing lagoon of blue which is beyond the normal agricultural spectrum'. This description is very accurate, because a flax crop grown in a coombe-bottom can look surprisingly like a lake.

Sheep and Shepherding

Prior to the ploughing of the Downs, which to a great extent came about as a result of war effort during the Napoleonic War and two World Wars, the Downs in general remained sheepwalks and a frequently seen figure was the downland shepherd and his dog. Shortly before the First World War changed the entire rural scene A.G. Bradley recorded seeing such a shepherd near Ogbourne in *Round About Wiltshire* (1907):

> I came across a fine figure of a Wiltshire shepherd one morning recently standing out against the sky on the rampart of a British camp near Ogbourne, overlooking half the county. He was a quite ideal picture, his crook in his hand, his cloak beside him on the ground, and lying upon it a shaggy grey sheepdog, which eyed me suspiciously, while the steady crunching all around of what Thomson

> would have called his 'fleecy care' was the only audible sound upon the waste.

At about the same time W.H.Hudson made a study in depth of shepherds, their dogs, and shepherding practice in the South Wiltshire Downs for *A Shepherd's Life* (1910). This is one of the finest books on rural Wiltshire, and is equally relevant to shepherding in the Marlborough Downs.

From time immemorial during the entire period of the sheep and corn husbandry under which sheep were brought off the uplands and folded overnight in the arable fields to manure them with their dung, the shepherd had been an integral part of the downland scene; Aubrey records such a shepherd in the seventeenth century. Hudson's book ends with an expression of the heartfelt feelings of an old shepherd for the downland environment in which he had spent all his working life:

> I don't say that I want to have my life again, because 'twould be sinful. We must take what is sent. But if 'twas offered to me and I was told to choose my work, I'd say, Give me my Wiltshire Downs again, and let me be a shepherd there all my life long.

For long periods during lambing time these shepherds lived rough in the shepherd's huts which any one who walks in downland is likely to see. These relics of sheep husbandry were used from about the middle of the nineteenth century. Previously shepherds living out for several weeks at lambing time made do with a primitive shelter of thatched hurdles, but in about 1850 the movable shepherd's hut made its appearance and was soon widely used. This was a timber-framed shed-like structure mounted on a timber undercarriage with four cast-iron wheels. It was usually clad with corrugated iron and had a segmental corrugated iron roof. A stove was normally included for the comfort of the shepherd, with a stovepipe carried through the roof. This stove also provided heat and warm milk for ailing or rejected lambs. A bunk crossed the end of the hut away from the door, which was normally of the stable type with two leaves reached up a short flight of detachable steps. The stable door permitted ventilation without allowing lambs to fall out of the hut. At lambing times the hut was drawn out to the lambing fold and the shepherd took up residence for the several weeks when the ewes required constant attention.

The timing of their introduction in about the 1850s and their striking resemblance to the railway box waggon, for which they can easily be mistaken when parked in a farmyard, prompts me to suggest that the shepherd's hut may have been inspired by the railway guard's van, which was also provided with a heating stove. They also have some resemblance to the earlier wheeled bathing machine of the Georgian period, and are very similar to the mobile living huts which were part of the equipment of the steam tackle gangs which came on to the farms and may also have led to the idea for the shepherd's hut. Road mender's huts are also very similar, but these usually have a box chest slung under them for hand tools to be carried.

Despite the fact – revealed by the maker's plate which was often displayed on them – that they were made by any number of rural agricultural smiths, shepherd's huts reveal a remarkable uniformity of design. The catalogue of one of the principal Wiltshire makers R. & J. Reeves of Bratton, reveals that in 1905 their large version cost £26, their medium £23, and the smallest £18, with 'Carriage Paid to any station not exceeding 100 miles from Works' which was near Westbury. A stove complete with floor plate and smoke stack was an optional extra at £1.5s (£1.25p). His hut was very much the shepherd's private domain, and no one was normally allowed near it, perhaps because – as I have heard a shepherd confess – 'They were very useful in the courting season'.

Recently shepherd's huts have become less common in the Downs, for they are now reaching the end of their life and are falling into decay. There is still (2002) a derelict example a little south of Liddington Hill which has suffered a great deal of damage from the severe gales of the past few winters, and several are still used at lambing time at Aldbourne Warren Farm.

Shepherds were regarded as senior men on the farms, and were generally given practically a free hand by the farmers. Their long solitary absences on the Downs gave them much time for contemplation and they often read and taught themselves various recreations. Some studied the scriptures, some became musicians and others expert on the flora and fauna of the district, especially the small game!

The well-known writer and Wiltshireman Ralph Whitlock recalled that his father studied shorthand, music and history whilst he was a shepherd boy on the Wiltshire Downs, and at the age of fourteen had lambed a flock on the same hill above their village where he lambed a flock when eighty-four years of age. A good shepherd was respected by the community and was often regarded as a sage by the other villagers. Shepherding practice has now changed. In former times the needs of his sheep ruled absolutely the life of the shepherd, but today the commitment of the old shepherds to practically living with their flocks is no longer demanded. There is now no need for a shepherd to be buried with a hank of wool to explain to St. Peter his irregular attendance at church, for the modern shepherd no longer lives on the open Downs with his charges. He visits them intermittently, often driving a four-wheel drive vehicle or a cross-country buggy. On one occasion I saw a shepherd riding a motor cycle across the Marlborough Downs with his sheepdog riding pillion.

An interesting revival of sheep droving occurred in the Marlborough Downs in 1986 and I believe in several subsequent years. The shepherd at Temple Farms, Rockley, drove his sheep 'on the hoof' along the road to Marlborough Fair which was that year revived and held on Marlborough Common after a lapse of twenty years. This drove was over only four miles, but was believed to be the first case of sheep being driven to the fair for twenty-five years.

Stubble-burning

Reverting to arable farming, from autumn 1992 the stubble-burning which has been for so long an objectionable feature of the countryside and has inconvenienced many recreational users of the Marlborough Downs and sometimes damaged hedges and trees, was banned by law and alternative methods of incorporation or disposal of stubbles have had to be found. This is a considerable inconvenience to farmers, but no more shall we experience vast palls of smoke clouding the autumn landscape.

Liddington Hill from Smeathe's Ridge with stubble burning (October 1992)

Racehorse Training

Whilst Salisbury Plain has been used for the training of soldiers, the Marlborough Downs have for many years been used for racehorse training. Just as the elastic turf of the Downs provided the ideal surface for the racecourses, it is also excellent for training racehorses, and many training gallops are to be seen around Avebury, at Manton House near Old Eagle and south of Barbury Castle. At Beckhampton the celebrated Mr. Fred Darling ran one of the most famous stables of his time, which won several Derbys with Steve Donoghue and Gordon Richards riding for the stable. There Mr. Darling was succeeded by Mr. Noel Murless. Manton House is equally famous, having been owned by Mr. Robert Sangster, the international racehorse owner.

The Wroughton area at the north-west edge of the Downs was also notable for training horses. One of the Wroughton public houses is named after the great Brown Jack which was foaled in 1924, was trained at Wroughton by Mr. Ivor Anthony, and was schooled over hurdles at

Barbury. In 1928-30 Brown Jack achieved the rather unusual distinction of winning major races both on the flat and over hurdles. Racehorses were also trained at Aldbourne and at Fox Hill east of Liddington Hill, and Bayardo Farm – south of West Woods – is named after a racehorse.

In 1991 a racecourse was created towards Barbury Castle with a view to holding four meetings every year, commencing in May 1992. Around Barbury Castle point-to-point race meetings have for some time been held, and the owners of the site of Snap village were at one time equine enthusiasts who erected jumps at Snap village site where they occasionally held events. There is also a riding centre above Rockley called the Marlborough Downs Riding Centre.

At a lonely spot on the Downs is to be found the private cemetery of the Hartigans, the Irish family who trained racehorses in the area and wished to be buried within the sound of the hoofbeats of the horses around which their lives had revolved. Several graves are contained within the tiny cemetery, the first being that of Patrick Frank Hartigan who died in 1921. On the pedestal of his Celtic cross is inscribed:

> 'Beneath the clean and spacious sky
> Here let the sleeping horseman lie,
> Nor from his darlings sunder;
> And as the thoroughbreds flash by
> This dust may quicken suddenly
> To hear the gallops thunder.'

Racehorses were trained at Rockley in the mid-nineteenth century by Mr. Edmund Jones. As a young man that most celebrated of jockeys Sir Gordon Richards lived in a bungalow near Rockley, and in later life returned to Stable Cottage at Rockley to train horses.

Sport and Recreation

In the last two decades of the nineteenth century and the first decade of the twentieth, when it was part of the Meux estates, Fyfield Down was preserved as a sporting estate. Pheasants, partridges and hares were encouraged alongside the rabbits of the warren, and parties of sportsmen took part in shoots on a grand scale by invitation. Wroughton Copse –

which is ancient woodland – Totterdown Woods, and Delling Copse which was planted in the nineteenth century as a game covert, were preserved for game, and lines of larch were planted to ensure that the birds rose over the guns. The rabbits of the warren were also shot. Shooting began in November when the rabbits were in their prime,and continued until January when it stopped to allow the rabbits respite to breed. On one notable occasion 4,000 rabbits were shot by six guns in a single day; 5,000 to 6,000 rabbits were killed each year on Fyfield Down Warren.

Two golf-courses exist at present in these Downs. Marlborough golf club is situated between Marlborough and Ogbourne Maizey, and only three miles to the north Swindon golf course occupies the western slopes of Round Hill Downs at Ogbourne St. George. A third course at Broome Manor north of Hodson is just outside the Marlborough Downs.

Illegal coursing of hares with fast dogs over open country is on the increase. In order to enjoy this sport its participants will travel long distances to reach suitable terrain. Large sums of money sometimes change hands in bets on the outcome, and the dogs are sometimes illegally followed across country in four-wheel-drive vehicles. On one occasion a farmer in the nearby Berkshire Downs measured wheel tracks amounting to over three miles through his standing corn in a single field. It is unfortunately now very evident that urban crime is spilling over into the countryside.

A recent 'official' recreational facility is the Barbury Castle Country Park which was created in the early 1970s to provide facilities for the public – and particularly the population of the rapidly expanding town of Swindon five miles to its north – to enjoy the countryside. Access is excellent by way of a good minor road running south from Burderop between Wroughton and Chisledon. A vast car park is provided together with public toilets, and the country park provides a good starting point for walks in the Marlborough Downs.

Flying

Between the two World Wars Wroughton aerodrome was constructed south of Wroughton and north-west of Barbury Castle. Apart from an occasional flying display it is now not much used as an aerodrome. Its vast hangars now house part of the collection of the Science Museum in London, and periodically events are held here connected with the museum.

Also near Wroughton, beside the turnpike road which runs past Barbury to Marlborough, was formerly the Princess Alexandra Royal Air Force Hospital. This survives as a jumble of buildings of various styles and periods which are generally not obtrusive, except for a large block which in my opinion (and I speak as an architect) commits the unpardonable sin of being a large glaring-white building in an Area of Outstanding Natural Beauty. It is visible in all its brash white assertiveness for miles around. At the entrance to this hospital for long stood a Gloster Meteor, a representative of the first British jet aircraft to see active service in the Second World War (and this flew only fifty-eight years after Richard Jefferies died!) but this was removed in 1991.

Fortunately none of the antiquities of the Marlborough Downs has ever – to my knowledge – been subjected to the threat of demolition because it lay on a flight path, as was Stonehenge in the early days of the Royal Flying Corps.

Farmers are now tending to make use of light aircraft and a private grass landing strip has been provided at Draycot Foliat, a place which has a link with Jefferies since some of his ancestors, including his great grandfather Richard Jefferies (c1734-1822) who bought Coate Farm where the writer was born, came from Draycot Foliat. It was of this parish that it was said there was ne'er a wife, 'ne'er a child, ne'er a cow, and ne'er a pig', the saying being explained by the fact that at Draycot Foliat lived three farmers called Jefferies, Neale and Puckeridge, all on arable farms worked by bachelor labourers with no cattle or pigs.

A modern development in these Downs is hang-gliding which generally takes place from Tan Hill, Martinsell, or the north-west face of Golden Ball Hill. Its popularity here is explained by the fact that the Wiltshire Hang Gliding Centre is based at Lockeridge, and it is claimed that the Marlborough Downs provide some of the best training slopes in the country.

Ordnance Survey

When the Ordnance Survey decided on a new survey of England in the early 1930s one of the principal base-lines for their triangulation was a line approximately seven miles long which ran between the trigonometrical points on Liddington Hill and on Uffington Hill. If a straight line is drawn between these two points it will be found that the Ridgeway nearly coincides with it, never departing more than a quarter of a mile from the straight line.

Experimental Earthwork

Another occurence of recent times was the construction in 1960 of the experimental earthwork on Overton Down (129 707) above Avebury. This project was undertaken at the instigation of the British Association for the Advancement of Science. A bank and ditch were constructed in order that the effects of natural weathering and soil erosion on an earthwork in a downland situation could be studied to further our knowledge about similar effects upon prehistoric earthworks. Artefacts of different material were buried within the earthwork. Periodically these are examined and the earthwork is sectioned to ascertain the effects of weathering and soil erosion.

The experimental earthwork on Overton Down, constructed in 1960 to observe the effect of natural erosion on earthworks.

Crop Circles

Having commenced my study of the history and landscape of the Marlborough Downs by referring to the ancient mysteries about the purposes for which the Neolithic monuments of Avebury and Silbury were created, I shall now end my survey of recent developments in these Downs by discussing the crop circles which are the great enigma of modern times. These geometrical patterns began to appear in numbers in the mid-1980s. They are by no means confined to Wiltshire but many crop circles appear annually in the Marlborough Downs in June, July and August, and almost always in cornfields. In 1991 at least eight complicated groups appeared in this area, two at Alton Barnes, three between Marlborough and Hackpen Hill, one under the west slope of Hackpen where the road descends the hill, one north of Barbury Castle, and one immediately west of West Woods. The numbers seem to increase every year. The phenomenon has been subjected to considerable scientific investigation and even Japanese scientists have become involved. To date crop circles have not been satisfactorily explained.

The most usual explanation – which has its passionate adherents – is that crop circles are caused by meteorological conditions, generally air turbulence, but other more frivolous theories such as hedgehogs, rutting roe deer and alien visitors have been advanced. Several books have been published attempting to explain crop circles and illustrating by photographs the great variety of shapes and combinations which have appeared.

The early examples tended to consist of one dominant large circle with four smaller satellite circles at cardinal points very precisely positioned. The later examples in the Marlborough Downs have been linear arrangements of four or five circles, aligned along a spinal bar. Each year the configurations are getting progressively more elaborate as they incorporate concentric circles and straight-sided geometrical shapes such as triangles.

Everyone loves a mystery and crop circles generate great interest. People flock to see them and they have become a tourist attraction. When they appear word rapidly gets around by radio, local press and the national press which gives the subject extensive coverage. The landowners often exploit the circles by charging admission to the fields in which they appear, but the circles are almost invariably in prominent positions visible from roads and footpaths. Nevertheless, many pay for the experience of walking in the circles and people have been known to camp overnight in them, with no known adverse consequences! In 1991 there occurred a case of opportunists who were not the landowners levying a charge for admission! There is a flourishing local trade in books and postcards, and local publicans sell key-rings and name their bar snacks after the crop circles.

Crop circles are fairly easily made with a stick as a centre, a length of rope and something such as sheets of hardboard to strap to the feet to avoid leaving footmarks. A garden roller also comes in useful, and there is no doubt that some are man-made hoaxes. One of the leading scientific investigators of the phenomenon has admitted that he has been misled into accepting some hoax circles as genuine.

As an unscientific and casual observer of crop circles, I have long held the decided opinion that all crop circles are man-made hoaxes, although I must admit that if this is the case the vast number which appear each year imply that a great number of people have lost a great deal of sleep creating them. The hoax explanation pours cold water on an interesting mystery and does not gain much credence with enthusiasts – including farmers and publicans! – who would prefer the lucrative mystery to remain unsolved.

The Future: Cause for Concern

Anyone who indulges in prophecy invites ultimate ridicule, but it seems evident that the landscape of the Marlborough Downs will continue to be subjected to pressures and that, as the drive for increased food production slackens, those pressures will come from the growing demands of recreational users. It is inevitable that the Downs will change, for no landscape ever remains static and unaltered. Man made this landscape, and man will change it, but it is to be hoped that the winds of change will not destroy the beauty of the Marlborough Downs.

These remain beautiful but they are under pressure first because man has lost his former apparently instinctive ability to improve the landscape by his actions, and secondly because the motor car has made even the remote areas accessible to vast numbers of an increased population which wishes to resort to the Downs for recreation. The particular problem of the Countryside Commission is that by promoting the Marlborough Downs as a recreational facility it may destroy its attractions, for it is inevitable that people in large numbers destroy what they most admire. As part of the North Wessex Downs, the Marlborough Downs have been declared one of thirty-eight Areas of Outstanding Natural Beauty and this designation was confirmed in 1972. The Countryside Commission recognises – and I quote from its 1990 'Policy Statement for Areas of Outstanding Natural Beauty' – that 'the quality of both the environment and of the tourist experience can be threatened by excessive and intensive tourism'. The Commission also stipulates that the promotion of tourism 'should be primarily aimed at those activities which draw on the character of the countryside itself, its beauty, culture, history, and wildlife'.

During the years that I was a Ridgeway Warden in the Marlborough Downs I sometimes saw the effects of appalling behaviour by a minority of people. It must be recognised that the recreational use of an area as sensitive as the Marlborough Downs brings with it an obligation to act responsibly, to treat the countryside with respect, and to recognise the interests of other people who use the countryside, particularly the people who use it as their workplace. It is imperative that this magnificent landscape shall be allowed by its present users to survive in a condition for people in the future to enjoy, just as past generations bequeathed it to us.

Fortunately irresponsible behaviour by a few individuals normally has only a short term impact. Far more important because of their long term implications are proposals for building developments in sensitive areas. In 1990 an application for a hotel was made for the extremely sensitive site of the transport cafe beside the Ridgeway on Overton Hill. This proposal was refused after considerable controversy which included some support for the proposal from local people. Development in a World Heritage Area is by no means a local issue, and it is encouraging that this proposal triggered national awareness to the extreme vulnerability of the Marlborough Downs to commercial interests. The National Trust acquired more land around Avebury, demolished the transport cafe and returned its site to grass. Recent events suggest that now that this country is within the European Community another tier of protection for sensitive landscapes is in place. In 1991 the Community revealed its willingness to interfere with controversial proposals on conservation grounds. It is to be hoped that the worst excesses will be prevented either as a result of public concern or as a result of action by the Government or the European Community.

Sarsens and thorns on Overton Down

The Ridgeway beckons walkers on over its little twists, risings and fallings as it runs north-east along Hackpen Hill

10 Walks in the Marlborough Downs

The most popular walk in the Marlborough Downs is along the Ridgeway which has been designated a Long Distance Trail by the Countryside Commission. For much of its length the Ridgeway is also a 'byway open to all traffic' and the Countryside Commission's promotion of the route, together with the in my opinion mistaken policy of surfacing long stretches of the Ridgeway with stone, has increased the usage of the Ridgeway by walkers, riders and wheeled traffic.

Fortunately, there are a great many alternative walks in the Marlborough Downs which are not subjected to such pressures and the following walks are suggested as an introduction to these Downs, and as a means of seeing for the first time their principle attractions. Each walk covers a distance from five to nine miles, which can comfortably be achieved in a day by anyone who is reasonably fit.

No maps are included as they would be poor substitutes for the Ordnance Survey maps. The relevant numbers of the Landranger and Explorer series of maps are indicated on each walk sheet. The Landranger maps are quite adequate for walking and two of these maps (Sheets 173 and 174) cover all the walks. Some walkers prefer the larger scale of the Explorer series, in which case one map (Explorer Sheet 157) covers most of the Marlborough Downs. All of the walks are circular and finish at the start point.

Where items are indicated under 'Note' in the walk directions information on that subject may be obtained by reference to the index.

1 Marlborough Downs

Distance: 9 miles

Maps Landranger 173 or Explorer 157

This walk provides a good general introduction to the landscape of the Marlborough Downs as it takes a circuit around the rim of the saucer of downland south of Barbury Castle.

Park at Barbury Castle car park (156 761) 5 miles S of Swindon and signposted from Wroughton and Chiseldon.

1. Walk SE then S down the turnpike road to Old Eagle (168 715). *Note:* Turnpike, Milestones, Four Mile Clump, Training gallops, Old Eagle.

2. At Old Eagle turn W through Rockley village.

3. At 158 720 follow the lane SW along the beech avenue and at 157 716 turn W.

4. Continue W taking right fork through sarsen stones to Old Totterdown (139 718).

5. Proceed NW through Totterdown Woods.

6. Walk NW past Glory Ann (128 726) to join the Ridgeway on Hackpen Hill at 125 730.

7. Continue N and NE along the Ridgeway above the Hackpen White Horse, crossing the minor road at 129 747.

8. Follow the Ridgeway as it descends and swings E. *Note:* Romano-British burial.

9. Cross another minor road at 146 764 and climb the track E to Barbury Castle hillfort. Note: Battle of Beranburh.

10. Follow the S ramparts of the hillfort to 152 763 enjoying the wide views across the Marlborough Downs to Martinsell to the S.

11. Continue E to the start point at the car park. *Note:* From the car park a short walk E will take you to the Jefferies Memorial Stone (159 763) which overlooks the site of Burderop Racecourse.

2 Fyfield Down

Distance: 7 Miles
Maps: Landranger 173 or Explorer 157
This walk takes in Fyfield Down, a particularly interesting area of prehistoric landscape which is missed by many visitors to the Avebury area.

Park in Avebury village.

1. Walk E out of Avebury up Green Street to the Ridgeway at 125 708.

2. Here turn N and follow the Ridgeway for about a mile to point 126 725.

3. From this point look SSW for a sight of the top of Silbury Hill just visible over Waden Hill.

4. Turn NE and walk the hedgeless path the short distance to Glory Ann (128 726).

5. From Glory Ann proceed SE through Totterdown Woods (137 719) *Note:* Sarsen stones.

6. At 143 714 where you meet a gravel track turn SW down this track which is the Old London Road, passing through the Fyfield Down Celtic field systems and past Delling Cottage. *Note:* Rabbit warrening.

7. Continue W up The Gangway (131 709) and cross the Ridgeway at 125 708.

8. Return to Avebury down Green Street which was the Old London Road.

Old London Road (left) over Fyfield Down

3 Liddington Hill, Upper Upham and Snap

Distance: 9 miles

Maps: Landranger 174 or Explorer 157

The north-east corner of the Marlborough Downs is covered by this walk which includes Sugar Hill, Liddington Hill, Upper Upham, and the deserted village of Snap.

Park in one of two lay-bys at Shipley Bottom (230 786) three miles NW of Aldbourne on the B4192 (formerly the A419 and so marked on old maps).

1. Walk E from 231 785 along the track and uphill on to Sugar Hill. *Note:* Site of rabbit warrens and views SW to Upham.

2. Near the ridge of Sugar Hill (237 787) turn NW at the farm gate and continue for about a mile and half to the road at 218 804. The path is not well-defined over the latter part of this stretch and it may be best to follow field margins.

3. At 218 804 cross the road (carefully) and climb the trackway which runs SW towards Liddington Hill.

4. From 213 797 follow the 'permissive' path (not signposted) NW and SW along field margins to Liddington hillfort and walk around the ramparts to the SW corner (207 796) where Jefferies used to sit.

5. Return to the Ridgeway path (at 213 797) and walk S for a mile and a half to the intersection of trackways (213 774) above Lower Upham

6. At the crossways turn E to UpperUpham and continue to see Upper Upham Manor House (229 772). *Note:* Upham deer park, Civil War.

7. Return short distance E and at 228 770 walk S down Haydown Drove to 227 764.

8. At this point turn W and follow field margin and lane to Snap deserted village (224 764).

9. Continue W out of Snap to the Ridgeway at 213 765.

10. Walk N for one mile along the Ridgeway to the fork at 214 780.

11. Take the right fork and proceed NE then E through Shipley Bottom to the start point.

4 Smeathe's Ridge and the Ogbournes

Distance: 8 miles
Maps:Landranger 173 or Explorer 157
This walk descends Smeathe's Ridge, passes the Ogbourne villages, and returns up the turnpiked road past Four Mile Clump.

Park at Barbury Castle car park (156 761) 5 miles S of Swindon and signposted from Wroughton and Chiseldon.

1. Walk E down Smeathe's Ridge taking care to turn left through the gate on the turnpike after a short distance (at 158 758).
2. Follow Smeathe's Ridge to the W end of Ogbourne St. George (at 193 747) enjoying the views ahead to Liddington Hill and Whitefield Hill and S to Martinsell.
3. At 193 747 turn S and for a very short distance follow the tarmac road and then take the old droveways for one and a half miles past Southend to Ogbourne St. Andrew. *Note:* Barrow in churchyard at Ogbourne St. Andrew.
4. From Ogbourne St. Andrew continue S along fieldpath across open fields parallel to the A345 to Ogbourne Maizey. *Note:* Manor House.
5. Here turn W and follow Drove Lane to the Downs to join the turnpike road at 168 731.
6. Follow the turnpike N past Four Mile Clump back to start. Note: Milestones.

Martinsell (left) and Four Mile Clump from Smeathe's Ridge

5 Martinsell, Oare and Huish

Distance: 9 miles

Maps: Landranger 173 or Explorer 157

The outward part of this walk follows the south escarpment of the Marlborough Downs above Pewsey Vale to Martinsell, and the return is through the villages under the escarpment.

Park in the Workway Drove (116 638) near Knap Hill on the minor road between Alton Barnes and Lockeridge.

1. Walk a short distance SE down the drove track and then cross the stile on the top of the bank to your left (118 635) and cross Knap Hill. From the hill enjoy the views E along the S escarpment of the Marlborough Downs, and W to Adam's Grave on Walker's Hill.

2. From Knap Hill continue W along the escarpment over Golden Ball Hill, and Draycot Hill and follow the N edge of Gopher Wood to point 143 645.

3. From this point a diversion of about half a mile each way to the NW may be taken to see the deserted village of Shaw. *Note* that the first section of the footpath (143 646 to 142 647) has for long been ill-defined and remained so in October 1992.

4. From 143 645 continue E forking right to Huish Hill and after crossing the A 345 (at 164 643) continue E over Oare Hill and up lane to Ravensgate (169 641).

5. Proceed E along the S side of Withy Copse (174 642) to Martinsell hillfort and walk clockwise around the ramparts enjoying the panoramic views.

6. From the SW corner of Martinsell hillfort walk SW past the old barn site and over Giant's Grave, descending steeply to 162 628 and follow the lane into Oare village.

7. Cross the A345 and continue W out of village by fieldpaths to Huish village. *Note:* 'The Ghost of Pit Pond'.

8. Continue N out of Huish past the pond and church and continue up hill to point 143 645 N of Gopher Wood where the outward route is rejoined.

9. Follow the route W back over Knap Hill to start.

6 Wansdyke and Tan Hill

Distance: 9 miles
Maps: Landranger 173 or Explorer 157
The glories of Wandsdyke are experienced on this walk, which also takes in Tan Hill Fair site.

Park at Overton Hill (119 681) on the N side of the A4 one mile E of Silbury Hill. *Note:* Silbury Hill, Barrow cemetery, The Sanctuary.

1. Follow the Ridgeway S to the River Kennet at 120 676. Note: Battle of Overton Hill.

2. Cross the footbridge and continue S through East Kennett Village.

3. At 121 671 leave the road taking the right fork up the track (the Ridgeway) past the farm and continue S to Wansdyke at Red Shore (118 648). *Note:* Adam's Grave ahead, Knap Hill, Battles of Wodnesbeorg, and Wansdyke.

4. Follow Wandsdyke W passing N of Oxenmere (106 641) which is worth a diversion although there is no official public footpath.

5. Continue W along Wansdyke as far as Tan Hill (082 653).

Note: Tan Hill Fair.

6. Return along Wansdyke as far as point 099 647.

7. Here turn NE and descend footpath to 114 677 noting the views towards Avebury and Silbury Hill.

8. At 114 677 turn E and cross the minor road at the bridge (116 677) and follow the footpath E along the N side of the river to point 120 676 near the footbridge which was crossed on the outward walk.

9. Here turn N up Overton Hill to the start point.

***Note**:* Take particular care when driving out of the parking place on to the A4 as traffic approaches very rapidly from the W and the visibility is particularly poor.

7 Silbury Hill and West Kennett Long Barrow

Distance: 5 miles.
Maps: Landranger 173 or Explorer 157
The archaeological field monuments of Silbury Hill, West Kennett Barrow and The Sanctuary are visited on this walk, which returns along a section of the Ridgeway.

Park in Avebury village.

1. Walk south from the main car park through point 099 696 and along the E bank of the winterbourne to opposite Silbury Hill.

2. Continue S, carefully crossing the A4 at 104 684 near Swallowhead Springs.

3. Take a short diversion on S to West Kennett long barrow which should on no account be missed.

4. Return to 104 682 and follow the footpath E past West Kennett Farm and then S through the fields to 114 677.

5. Here turn E, cross the minor road near the bridge at 116 677, and follow the footpath E along the N side of the River Kennet to 120 677.

6. Turn N and walk up the slope of Overton Hill to the A4. *Note:* Battle of Overton Hill, The Sanctuary.

7. Cross the A4 and follow the Ridgeway past the Barrow Cemetery on Overton Hill.

8. Continue N up the Ridgeway for half a mile to 119 688.

9. Here take the path which runs W from the Ridgeway, and then continue NW to Green Street at 111 703.

10. Follow Green Street – which was formerly the Old London Road – W into Avebury.

As an alternative, or even better as an addition to the above walks, no one should hesitate to take their maps and follow rights-of -ways into any part of the Marlborough Downs. To use the words of Timperley in *Ridge Way Country*: '....do not fall into the mistake of thinking that seven league boots are needed for the discovery of downland pleasures'. Access is good , and the rewards are great.

FURTHER READING

Geology

R.S. Barron: *The Geology of Wiltshire* (Moonraker Press, 1976)

Isobel Geddes: *Hidden Depths: Wiltshire's Geology & Landscapes* (Ex Libris Press, 2000)

Topography

H.W. Timperley: *Ridge Way Country* (Dent, 1935)

H.J. Massingham: *The English Downland* (Batsford, 1936)

E. Thomas: *Richard Jefferies: His Life and Work* (1909; Faber, 1978)

Brentnall and Carter: *The Marlborough Country* (Oxford, 1932)

Flora and Fauna

Arlott, Fitter & Fitter: *The Complete Guide to British Wildlife* (Collins, 1981) – a general book for the rucksack covering most wildlife, flora and fauna.

D.J. Grose: *The Flora of Wiltshire* (EP Publishing reduced facsimile, 1979)

J. Buxton: *The Birds of Wiltshire* (Wiltshire Library and Museum Service, 1981)

Archaeology and History

L.V. Grinsell: *The Archaeology of Wessex* (Methuen, 1958)

P.J. Fowler: *Wessex* (Regional Archaeology Series: Heinemann, 1967)

G. Osborn: *Exploring Ancient Wiltshire* (Dorset Publishing Co., 1982)

The Wiltshire Archeological Magazine (referred to as WAM in my text)

The Victoria County History (referred to as VCH in my text)

Ken Watts: *Exploring Historic Wiltshire Vol. 1: North* (Ex Libris Press, 1997)

Communications

Timperley and Brill: *Ancient Trackways of Wessex* (Dent, 1965 and Drinkwater, 1983)

K.G. Watts: *Droving in Wiltshire: the trade and its routes* (Wiltshire Life Society; 1990)

K.R. Clew: *The Kennet and Avon Canal* (David & Charles, 1968)

L.J. Dalby: *The Wilts & Berks Canal* (Oakwood Press, 1971)

Barrett, Bridgeman & Bird: *A Midland and S.W. Junction Railway Album* (Red Brick Publishing, 1981)

Villages

K.G. Watts: *Snap: the History, Depopulation and Destruction of a Wiltshire Village* (Wiltshire Library and Museum Service, 1989)

Writers

E. Thomas: *Richard Jefferies: His Life and Work* (1909; Faber, 1978)

L. Clark: *Alfred Williams: His Life and Work* (David & Charles, 1969)

M. Wilson: *Charles Hamilton Sorley: a biography* (Cecil Woolf, 1985)

Walking

N. Curtis: *The Ridgeway National Trail Guide* (Arun Press, 1989)

J.R.L. Anderson and Fay Godwin: *The Oldest Road: An Exploration of the Ridgeway* (Whittet Books, 1975)

Ken Watts: *Exploring Historic Wiltshire Vol. 1: North* (Ex Libris Press, 1997)

INDEX

Chapter 10: Walking (pp 173-180) and Further Reading (pp 181-182) are omitted from this index, as are places distant from the Marlborough Downs. Illustrations are indexed with page numbers in italics.

More books of Wiltshire interest from Ex Libris Press:

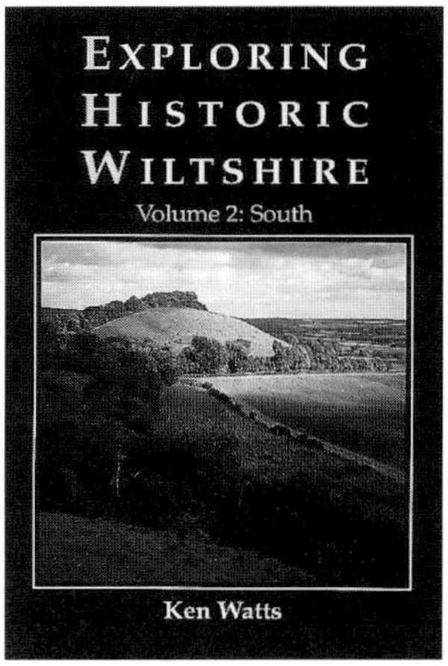

EXPLORING HISTORIC WILTSHIRE
Volume 2: South
by Ken Watts
Featuring six of the finest landscapes of rural south Wiltshire

176 pages; Illustrated
ISBN 0 948578 92 0
Price £7.95

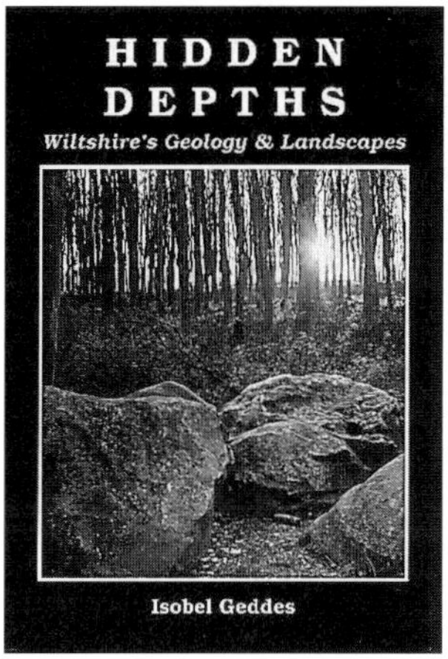

HIDDEN DEPTHS:
Wiltshire's Geology and Landscapes
by Isobel Geddes

224 pages; Illustrated throughout with photographs, maps and cross-sections.
ISBN 1 903341 05 1
Price £9.95

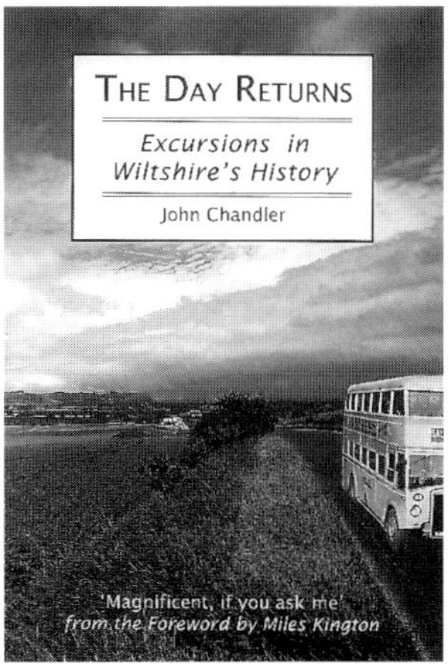

THE DAY RETURNS
Excursions in Wiltshire's History
by John Chandler
This is the perfect dipping into book for all lovers of Wiltshire

256 pages; Illustrated
ISBN 0 948578 95 5
Price £9.95